SPRING 65

A JOURNAL OF

ARCHETYPE

AND

CULTURE

Spring and Summer, 1999

SPRING JOURNAL

WOODSTOCK, CONNECTICUT 06281

Contents

ACKNOWLEDGMENTS

To Princeton University Press for quotations from the *Collected Works (CW)* of C. G. Jung (Bollingen Series XX), translated by R. F. C. Hull, edited by Herbert Read, Michael Fordham, G. Adler, and William McGuire, and published in Great Britain by Routledge and Kegan Paul, London. Other quotations have been acknowledged throughout in appropriate notes and references.

Spring is printed in Canada, text on acid-free paper.

Spring is the oldest Jungian journal in the world. It was founded in 1941 by the Analytical Psychology Club of New York. In 1970, James Hillman transferred its editing and publication to Zürich, Switzerland. From 1978 to 1988, it was edited in Dallas, Texas. Since 1988 it has been edited in Connecticut. Jay Livernois is the publisher.

The majority of my patients consisted not of believers but of those who had lost their faith. The ones who came to me were the lost sheep.

C. G. Jung

Editors' Note

It used to be that lost souls simply went to Hell and that was that. If they did not reform, it was their own damn (and damning) fault. Nor were lost souls part of the grand picture that Renaissance thinkers gave us when they first invented a modern discourse on soul and soul-making. Michelangelo himself cast a lot of them down off the lofty ceilings of the Sistine Chapel—they were, as always, not beautiful enough. Even the Greeks who invented the word psyche simply laughed at the masses of helpless, broken, ugly humanity who could not live the examined life that gave the privileged their great soul features and gave everybody else their problems.

Today, fortunately, lost souls get a little more compassion. There are all kinds of psychological help programs available to them, from Alcoholics Anonymous meetings to Internet chat rooms on obesity. (Indeed, cyberspace is more and more the place for every human weakness.) In these programs people's feelings get soothed—and with new drugs it is easier than ever—but what about their souls?

Spring has not always been, we confess, a soul journal for such people. From our refined beginnings in the 1940s among a group of elegant Jungian women in New York to our higher Renaissance god and goddess issues of the 1970s and 80s, we have not given much time to the truly lost among us. (For one thing, with their Attention Deficit Disorders and what have you, we thought they did not read!—although we did do an issue called *Disillusionment* once and it sold out twice before we knew it.) This issue, with our apologies for past neglect, is for them.

But it is not the problems of the lost that we concentrate on, nor the remedies, solutions, or reforms of behavior. As always, we try to contemplate their souls, to see if reconnecting people to their lost psyches is not of more importance today than mere symptom alleviation. As Edward Tick, who works with post-traumatic stress syndrome patients (especially those still suffering from the Vietnam War), writes, "brutality has chased the soul from its connections to this world." Tick listens to an ex-Marine who tells him his soul is sitting next to him, and he cannot get it back. And Tick is the first psychologist, the man says, who ever seems to have understood what that might even means.

John Burns (whose last contribution here was in *Spring 61: Haiti, or the Psychology of Black*) seems to take the same approach in dealing with alcoholics and addicts. Having found the usual Alcoholics Anonymous route less than rewarding—teenagers especially do not want to hear about it—he took up the practice of archetypal psychology, virtually inventing its application to this kind of group therapy. His work is particularly striking because it deals with a population (Brazil's) that lives at the edge of traditional Western monotheism, and that knows polytheism far more instinctively than the rest of us.

On the other hand, do not think Jungian therapists are always the place to go with soul problems. Karen Hodges, a Jungian analyst herself, argues that while women are more inclined to become lost souls than men—statistics showing they are more depressed—they get lost in even another sense, for women who go to Jungian analysts, she claims, lose their souls yet a second time to Jung's outdated and highly prejudiced anima/animus scheme.

But even psychology itself may not be the ultimate focus for lost souls. Mike Denney, who is a surgeon, writes of patients who get liver transplants and who suddenly become obsessed with the idea that they now have someone else's soul inside them. This is taking the soul more literally than we ever imagined possible, but Denney gives case after case of the phenomenon.

In his amazing article on onanism—masturbators were once considered the truly lost souls of history—Patrick Singy shows the various bizarre fantasies that scholars, clergy, and the medical profession have had about it over the centuries, especially in the past two hundred years. Yet one cannot help wondering if medical science is not taking the same silly view today of contemporary lost souls—all the little boys forced to take Ritalin when they misbehave, the obese who are subject to precise doses of some dietician's highly arbitrary food pyramid, the alcoholic who has to swear by a twelve-step program, and so on.

Nonetheless, medical problems and clinical solutions are not the subject here. Soul is. As always, it is found in the strangest places, perhaps only in the strangest places. And finding it is what *Lost Souls* is all about.

— The Editors

Letters to the Editors

"Sometimes a Cigar is just a Cigar"

To the Editors, *Spring Journal*:

May I ask for space to comment on the passages in the excellent interview with Toni Frey in *Histories* (*Spring 64*), an altogether superb issue of your journal. In particular I want to address his account of his betrayal by C. A. Meier and his ejection from the *Klinik am Zürichberg* which Toni Frey originated and was its devoted leader. I write this both in defense of an old companion, Toni Frey, (and also to put down an old enemy, C. A. Meier), and mainly to criticize Frey's account—not its veracity or its facts—for his method of psychological understanding. It exemplifies how psychology can distort, even pervert, ordinary human experience.

Toni Frey, with touching openness, states clearly (79) that the "Jung Clinic was destroyed by his [Meier's] action;" that their close relationship during some thirty years was irreparably broken; that it was "one of the worst" moments of his [Frey's] life (81).

Why not call a spade a spade? Why not come out and say that Meier was brutal, false, unloving, and decidedly unoriginal: these were some of his character traits. Although I state this after many years of personal relations with him and my sometimes privileged and embroiled witness to the Zürich scene between 1953 and 1978, my argument draws its evidence from Toni Frey's own words (80): "...the thing with Meier exploded with the issue of our daughter being involved in the Zürich riots...and...had been beaten up by a policeman, and he said, 'whoever goes into danger will be hurt.' ... It was not the reaction I expected from a friend."

As the interviewer says, Meier blamed the victim, showed no sympathy for the beaten girl or his "friend's" fatherly feeling, distanced himself with a banality, and apparently took the side of the police (to which I can attest from my conversations with Meier on the Zürich riots in which at least one of my daughters, too, was involved.)

There was a second issue between them: the Clinic. The *Spring* interview says Meier wanted more and more money diverted to his research projects at the Clinic; Frey balked. I would like to hear more about this research, this money. How was it spent; on what? What were Meier's research results? From my experience with him in parapsychology research during some two years, I am suspicious. Our small group which he led (for which I raised the funds), and which included Frey and Alfred Ziegler, came up with zilch. Ziegler, who was a most cautious, perceptive, subtle, productive, and original person (some of his character traits) told me he believed Meier was doing this research for his own indulgence; he had scientific pretensions. Ziegler quit the group.

Despite these painful events for Toni Frey, events that reveal Meier's character, Frey's account doesn't call a spade a spade. He understands them with psychological language: the arrival of the shadow, repressed homosexuality, the daughter anima, imposing father figure, Oedipus dynamics, "the self in the form of Meier," and finally, *horribile dictu*: "...he did me a personal favor by kicking me out of the Clinic..." (78).

To Toni Frey's credit, his account shows compassion; mine, vengeance (character traits). Also, this pot should not call that kettle black, since I, too, often use psychological language. I would easily have explained Meier's behavior as classically senex. Saturn eats his children and has a female cohort, Lua, a devastating anima figure if there ever was one.

Instead, I am trying to set aside psychodynamic and archetypal approaches for something more direct, even if my move regresses to pre-psychological modes of perceiving people. Besides, I am not in the least interested now in analyzing Meier. "Mistah Kurtz—he dead" (epigraph to T. S. Eliot's "The Hollow Men"). Toni Frey made that clear: he really dead.

I am coming to the conviction, and to the point of this convoluted letter, that psychological explanation of human failing fails the human. Frey was ruthlessly treated and the Clinic betrayed: *basta*. As Eugene Monick says (writing of Clinton in *New Harmony Journal*, 15/1, 3, Pittsboro, North Carolina, 1999), he had a "really deep personal fault." Monick refrains from understanding Clinton in terms of an absent father, two mothers, sexual obsessions, shadow, power, etc. Nor does Monick make an archetypal move that would give Clinton's fault a mythical background in the divine right of kings. No, the President has a flaw in character, like any of us, like all of us, and character is destiny and irreparable. No exoneration, only contrition.

Unlike Toni Frey, I say: sometimes a cigar is just a cigar; a son of a bitch is a son of a bitch and not a Self symbol. Meier showed some of his character at that dinner. Like Marlow in Joseph Conrad's *Lord Jim*, at a critical moment Meier failed. Irreparable. *Basta.*

The poet David Whyte in a recent issue of the *Salt Journal* (2/2, 9, 2000) says:

> ...you have the jargon of, say, fundamental Christianity and of poetics and of the work world and of the New Age movement. And they are all equally pernicious because they do not speak to reality. They create a self-serving reality that is useful to that particular subgroup... But it's not language as a congress between ordinary people. It's one of the reasons I don't believe there are any good poets that have come out of the New Age movement, because the images are so clichéd... And the use of various phrases that have come from psychology have almost destroyed true compassion for another person... You no longer see a person but someone who is "dysfuntional," "alcoholic," "needy"...

Psychological language, and the understanding it supposedly brings, does not "speak to reality." No cigar. Psychology sees its own concepts, and psychologists "create a self-serving reality that is useful to that particular subgroup." The understanding Toni Frey finds—God bless him—in regard to a major tragedy in his life, the life of the Clinic and of Jungian therapeutic practice, has replaced the ordinary perception of reality.

I have long wondered why psychologists are so often off track in their judgements about people, even about their own intimates. I used to think it was part of the calling—to be especially obtuse in the ordinary world of spades and cigars. Now, however, I am coming to realize that we go off track because our perceptions of people are no longer phenomenal, and our judgements follow. We can "save the phenomenon" by seeing things as they are, but only if we say things as they are, naming characteristics accurately. To replace conceptualizations with characteristics is one reason I wrote my last two books, *The Soul's Code* and *The Force of Character.*

There are implications in this move toward a more phenomenal psychology that I have not even begun to work out, but Toni Frey's piece was so moving, so exemplary, and so disturbing that it has launched me into deep waters in an unfinished boat. But others are already going forward in this direction. Ginette Paris at Pacifica Graduate Institute and Maria-Teresa Colonna at the University of Florence are teaching psychological perception and understanding without using psychology's language. Instead they use literature and scenes from ordinary life, often with examples from pre-psychological times. The idea I am beginning to gather from them is this: psychologists, train your eye to perceive traits of character, and use the great, rich tradition of common speech and well-written prose to see the peculiarities of each specific human being.

James Hillman
January, 2000

Dear *Spring*,

Thank you for receipt of "Histories"—*Spring 64*—together with the latest catalogue. I've just finished reading Giegerich's article, which I found "deep," rich, complex, and extremely challenging to digest (at one go). Contentious as ever, I think the jury will be out for some time milling over the implications of what it means to develop the intellectual psyche at the expense of reading the world imaginatively. Did it not sound to you like a re-visitation of Plato's dialogues relating to the eternal Being (see *Timaeus*)? Anyway, I was amazed that this scholarly piece did not once refer to the "paradoxical" nature of existence—that up is down, left is right, and so forth. I think, in short, that he is taking the idea of depth too literally—which is what he is accusing archetypal psychology of having done. "Know thyself"—fine, but Wolfgang, "know thy shadow" also. I wait with interest to see what the repercussions will be of this "bombshell" of an article.

Steve Rawlinson
Devon, England

A Note on Hermes Inflation

JAMES HILLMAN

Despite our postmodern, polysemiotic, ironic, avant-garde, deconstructed, psychoanalytical sophistication, it is damned difficult for us to shed our historical monotheism. I once heard Karl Kerényi, who taught me mythology in Zürich almost fifty years ago, say it was impossible to return to the Greek style of mind. We cannot escape two thousand years of Christianism and its pervasive monotheistic psychology which favors an abstracting, cohesive, unifying, and centrally organizing viewpoint—or what psychology has baptized as "ego." We seem unable to escape obeisance to "one-sidedness" (Jung's definition of neurosis, by the way), which raises one or another perspective above all others. Thus it is not Hermes who has caught the psychology of our times but the perdurance of monotheism. Hermes and his computer is merely the fashionable front-man.

The shifts in gods influencing twentieth-century psychology do not indicate a true displacement of the monotheistic model in favor of a

James Hillman's latest book is *The Force of Character*, published by Random House. This essay was written as a response to Bernard Neville's characterizing Hillman as a Hermes type. Bianca Garufi and Pierre Denivelle translated and first published this piece in Italian.

polytheistic consciousness. One god rises to the foreground to vanquish all others and then subsides. For a while it was the Great Mother. Neumann, Bowlby, the Kleinians took over the entire pantheon. Earlier there was the dominance of the heroic ego: "where id was there ego shall be," draining the Zuyder Zee like Hercules cleaning the stables, resisting the regressive monsters and sirens of the id, like Ulysses tied to the mast, a good-enough husband heading home. We also have a monocular focus on Artemis and on the Amazons with anti-phallic combative feminism. And, we have had, or been had by, a one-sided identification with the abandoned child, victimized, abused, and sentimentalized.

These vagaries in the patterns of myth influencing psychological theory are merely slight twists in the same kaleidoscope of monocular vision. Each is a point of view, interpreting phenomena in terms of one God or Goddess only. Changing gods, their names, or their locations (from Judah to Attica) or gender (from upward phallic arrow to descending pubic cross) does nothing to the unifying insistence of Western Christianized consciousness (our cultural psyche) and its faith in singleness. The shift to Hermes is one more such turn, as if the contemporary psyche were desperately trying to writhe free from the Uroboros of Western History that swallows every emerging potential back into the same unifying loop. Remember what the patristic thought police said in their debates with the ancient polytheistic texts: "We take prisoner every thought for Christ." (Gregory of Nazianus)

Though Neville[1] admirably explicates the manner in which Hermes has become the one high God of the contemporary scene, dominating our world from market economics to information age communication, Neville's discussion remains monotheistic, willy nilly. For instance, when he accuses Hermetic consciousness of "radical relativism," he misses the psychological experience that while engaged in any conflict, there is no relativism. We are torn between calls; caught, challenged. There is emotional involvement, the immersion in the penetration by the issue at hand, called problem, conflict, ambivalence, opposites, whatever. The pathologized movement is always radical yet never relative.

[1] *Editors' note*: Bernard Neville is the professor of Humanistic and Archetypal Psychology in the School of Education, Latrobe University, Bundoora Campus, Victoria, Australia. His article appeared in the *Journal of Analytical Psychology*, 37, 1992, 337-353.

Only when stepping back and theorizing in the reflective stance about polytheistic consciousness can we speak about radical relativism. Only when one has assumed the old ego position of evaluation and choice outside the engagement of myth in life, then many alternatives can seem equally possible. Then one feels able to choose among the myths or the gods. But that posture too is mythical; consciousness is reflecting Hercules at the crossroads or unsure Paris asked to choose among the Goddesses, or enlightened Apollo musing at a distance. In other words, only the "ego" can speak of mythical complexity as "radical relativism," rather than as a dramatic tragedy or the constellation of fate.

The classical and Renaissance solution to identification with one God, i.e. the monotheistic affliction, was not resolved by syncretism or "getting it all together" by worshipping all gods, as if standing in a circle and bowing to each in turn. This keeps the old "I" in the center, apportioning attention according to the principle of equity (Apollo? Saturn and his scales? Athene and justice?...) A pantheon is a Roman idea, appearing in a culture that still today gives home to One True Universal Church (i.e. Catholic).

No, the Greek and Renaissance solution to identification with any single god was the profound realization that never does one god appear alone. The gods are not so much distinct units as interwoven patterns implicating one another. May I refer you here to *Re-Visioning Psychology*, Part III, but even more to one of its sources, Edgar Wind's chapter, "Pan and Proteus" in his masterful work *Pagan Mysteries of the Renaissance.* There he lays emphasis upon the duplicity if the gods and their inherent involvement with one another. He writes: "The mutual entailment of the gods was a genuine Platonic lesson." He recalls Schiller's verse: *Nimmer, das glaube mir, erscheinen did Götter, / Nimmer allein.* ("Never, believe me, never do the Gods appear alone.")

The myths place the gods always in *complicatio*, that is, necessary to one another often expressed as trinities. Hermes, for instance, could be "sided" with Dionysos, with Zeus his father, with Apollo his brother, and with his own underworld aspect. As well, he was linked with Hestia and Aphrodite. There was no single Hermes, standing like a bare white marble statue. The epithets of the gods portrayed and betrayed their affinities and polythematic complexities.

Besides, their myths have them squabbling, as Neville says. As we know from our own lives, squabbling is a major form of relating, of being involved with one another, especially where relationships are entangled as among families and close colleagues. To squabble is to be affected, afflicted, even infected by the other. Myths present patterns of contagion, and gods appear first in myths and rituals, only later as figures separated and hardened into symbols. Hermes cannot be singled out and treated alone without falling into a monotheistic consciousness which contradicts the very origin and nature of Hermes in the polytheistic cosmos. So, the Hermes we are indulging today is one fallen from the brotherhood and sisterhood. He is not in the limits of divine company. He has lost his association with the gods, become only profane.

There is no longer the ancient Hermes, the polytheistic Hermes, but a mercurial mask disguising the same old monotheism of our civilization. This Hermes offers neither help for the wayfarer nor guidance of souls, nor can he link human life to its depths in the Underworld and its Shades. Instead this Hermes is salesman of the usual salvation program and its grandiosity of hope and faith in progress to kingdom come, now by means of post-modern (de-)constructions, electronic universality, deregulated "free" marketing by players in the game, and invisible molecular recombinations. What Neville calls the inflation of Hermes is the conflation of Hermes with the secular and singular Western ego.

At risk of going on too long about a theme I have already written too much about in the course of too many years, I want to discern one crucial difference between an archetypal *psychology* and those writings with which Neville has placed mine (Lyotard, Foucault, Baudrillard, Maturana, Derrida) and make clear my alignment with Jung. Back to basics: because images are the primary mode of thinking and devotion in monotheism's pagan rivals, Hebrew, Christian, and Muslim psychology has been wary of image. "Image is psyche," said Jung. Moreover, Freud began depth psychology by investigating the dream image. This is the *via regina*, he said, the royal road for the return of the repressed.

Now, if images are essential to the pagan polytheism and are the stuff that monotheistic consciousness represses, and if images are the ways in which the repressed returns, then images are the mode by which the pagan psyche becomes visible, and sticking to them becomes the first step of a polytheistic method. Imagining better describes the method for engaging the repressed than analyzing into meaning or moralizing into positive and negative.

It further follows that conceptual language fails the image and the method of imagining. Therefore, terms Neville uses for critiquing Hermes consciousness, such as "relative," "multi-perspectivism," "positive and negative" drop from hermetic discourse while the search for a substantial "reality" apart from the image becomes vainly chimerical. Once we stick with the image, it draws us in, iconically fascinating, a resonance of souls. For, if image is psyche, then image is soul. (Do please note here, I use the word I gained the value of from Jung, a word hard to find in Lyotard, *et cie.* Hence, archetypal psychology is a psychology and not an exercise of the ironic French intellect.)

Despite the unfathomable depth (Heraclitus) to which an image opens and from which our more narrow and fearful consciousness tries to rescue the image by means of interpretive schema, we are solidly founded in a true reality when sticking with the image. It is psyche in its primordial originating shape. That's why archetypal psychology requires no foundation in another so-called reality and why it is not dependant upon an external philosophy, science or metaphysics. It relates to them and exchanges with them, as Hermes with his Olympian family and friends. But Baudrillard and Neville are quite right—the image requires for its significance no direct relation with any reality posited as more real, more foundational, than the image itself. For Psychology, the image *is* the thing itself. Even archetypes, gods and myths are knowable only as images.

Again, let us keep in mind the fact of our ingrained iconoclastic bias. Of course we have trouble grasping the nature of images. We fear them. We hate them. We kill them. Subliminally we know they are the ambassadors of alien gods. If conquering cultures reduced the threat of other gods by physically smashing images, psychology does the same work more subtly. We reduce the image to rationalistic explanations and personal history. If we cannot squeeze an acceptable meaning from an image—one that is coherent with our world view—we discard the image as meaningless and wait for the next dream to come along. By separating the image from its divine message, the analytical method for all its fawning on Hermes and hermeticism actually keeps him and all his company at bay.

To work through the Hermes inflation, we have first to restore Hermes to his polytheistic authenticity. This requires restoring images to their primary place as carriers of many kinds of divine messages. Hermes *psychopompos* transmitted the gods' messages by psychic means, via the soul, to the soul. Since images are souls per se, the medium of Hermes' message is the psychic image.

For us in practical psychology this means respecting the image as a *logos spermatikos*, a spark of divine intention, igniting imagination. The invisibility of Hermes the messenger within the image means that an image is neither a replica, a simulacrum, a representation, nor a derivative of any other reality. It generates out of nothing that we already know, which in no way assumes a nihilism, but rather an autochthonous source as myths themselves. An image calls out to imagination. Or, as Jung has said in his interpretive method: dream the myth along.

As Neville says, the grand narratives have been voided. They have been taken to the underworld; deconstructed, deliteralized, depotentiated. All the way down, neither turtle nor supportive elephant. We no longer look to big integrative ideas from, say Hegel, Teilhard de Chardin, Toynbee or even Einstein for living our lives. Hermes has taught us to treat ideologies hermeneutically (to meet them with suspicion) and hermetically (to search theories for their secretly hidden images). Hermes as God of invisibility has become Master of paranoia. And so all the old virtues of intellect prized by other gods (Saturn, Athene, Apollo, Metis, Zeus)—coherence, universals of explanation, laws of logic, axioms, verifications, and deep thoughtful construction—have become deceptions, a white, patriarchal, con game. Hermes-Mercurius who once was a God of the versatility of word and mind and writing is his undoing, deconstructing his own virtues, cheating the human world of any true grounding.

This leads Neville to say we are floating in a sea of images. However, suppose these images are life preservers after the shipwreck of titanic modernism, each grand narrative, such as Marxist economics, social Darwinism, Freudian Oedipal theory, is competitively more inclusive, more inflated than the next, each supposedly unsinkable as permanent truths.

Instead, suppose or imagine, each image floating by contains its depth, its story, and its values. We need but take hold of one and not let go, letting it prove the eternal buoyancy of myth and its beings. We have never given the image a chance to realize all it can offer in our iconoclastic culture, traces of which still besmirch even Neville's excellent article which speaks of images as "only" images. Have we not yet realized that all depth lies on the surface and that the gods display in detail, the phenomenon itself, and not the overreaching philosophy from which the profound and distinct eachness of the phenomenon must be saved. Images may keep us afloat in the actuality of life, our actual lives lived without fundamental anchor and without hope of being fished from the sea by some godly fisherman in the salvational net of a grand narrative.

***

Sometimes my polytheistic intoxication lets me imagine things from the other side. Then it seems to me that the gods have been deprived of images for so long that they have been going quite mad, finding only concepts and abstractions and formulae in which to settle down. And they are uncomfortable there. Not enough fun, not enough fantasy: too much definition, their *complicatio* and ambiguity too easily brought under human control.

I find myself believing that the immortals—as Greeks spoke of the gods—desire visibility among the mortals. They long for adequate images. Otherwise they remain literally invisible and are homeless on earth. They seem always to have an affinity with, and desire for, images. From the earliest cave paintings, history everywhere shows our recognition of their desire. Wherever humans have gone we set up their images to support our culture, much as we now set up electronic, media and mercantile images, as an impoverished way of honoring Hermes.

I like to believe that the gods in their frustration try in every which way to awaken our imagining capacities by forcing images upon us—in dreams, in fantasies, in memories, in fears and pornographies. Since the secular world no longer invites the gods into its images—having banned beauty from its schools of image-making and confined the invisible powers to "religious" art and art of the "insane" and their therapies—what can these powers do but press their presence upon us in distorted forms, such as the current obsessions with Hermes that Neville catalogues. Their description, their imageless homelessness drives them into the last place available: the human mind. As Heinrich Zimmer said years ago, "All the gods are within." And as Jung continued, "The gods have become diseases." Their insanity has become the root of ours.

A major sign of this insanity is the insane way our times uses the word "image." Having been severed from its immortal associations, it can be affixed to any transient mortal event from pixels to personas to pop pictures. Images require a cosmology that gives them value and holds them in order from within. That is why Vico said that the *vera narratio* ("true narrative") of myths are important for ordering the imagination.

At its beginning, depth psychology must surely have pleased the gods. It incited the repressed return. But the repressed returned within an utterly secular and scientific cosmology. Thus, Hermes, deprived of his depth and his divinity, became secularized, merely slippery, deceiving, seductive, commercial, a thief and a liar, as Neville writes, and his inventiveness and invisibility became scientized as electronic technology.

So, I imagine him to be urging us to find more valid images to hold the invisibles; he is asking to be freed of the glass and plastic alter of your PC monitor and be given a more welcomingly beautiful place on earth. The construction of such image receptacles means depth psychology must not fail the battle in the mind launched by Freud (against the illusion of religion) and Jung (against the one-sided Christ). This essential battle against Western history's monotheistic unconsciousness necessitates a battle against monotheism's professional minions of its secularism and scientism, today's thought-police, who, in the name of mental health and therapy of soul, apply ego psychology to the diseases of the gods.

Archetypal Psychology and Addiction Treatment

JOHN E. BURNS

Can archetypal psychology be used to help addicts? At Vila Serena, a chemical treatment center in Sâo Paulo, Brazil, the answer is "yes," although it was not an easy answer to come by. A highly motivated and inspired staff creates a compassionate therapeutic environment in which addicts can find their way to a perception of life worth living without psychoactive substances. We create the climate, and they find their way. The challenge is to motivate the professionals to become personally involved with the intractable problem of alcoholism and drug addiction.

In Brazil, we have been able to sustain a high level of morale and dedication among our treatment center personnel[1] by developing a pragmatic program based on our impressions of archetypal psychology. This has resulted in low employee turnover, a high occupancy rate and a reduction in relapses. When we started, sixteen years ago, we recommended that the addict surrender to a "Higher Power" or

[1] We operate twelve Minnesota model, inpatient, outpatient, and family program centers with about two hundred and fifty employees and have treated more than 25,000 dependents and their families. For more go to: www.vilaserena.com

John E. Burns, Ph.D., CEAP, is a former Roman Catholic priest, a member of Alcoholics Anonymous, founder and director of twelve chemical dependency treatment centers in Brazil, and a practitioner of archetypal psychology.

to "the God of your understanding" (as recommended by the Twelve Steps of Alcoholics and Narcotics Anonymous), attend a self-help group,[2] and read the literature. This method gave us about a thirty percent sobriety rate.[3]

We gradually recognized that sobriety was established by having a person in treatment repeatedly tell his or her story in a compassionate environment peopled with other addicts. Although this focus on the patient narrative seemed to help and we were aware that narrative is the basis of the popular "family systems theory,"[4] we lacked the confidence to focus our program on story because we did not yet perceive the philosophical underpinnings for this move. And, although the monotheistic, Christian nature of the Twelve-Step program is rejected by an increasing number of drug and alcohol dependents, especially adolescents,[5] we did not abandon the standard Twelve-Step program because it provided free meetings around the world and addressed religious and spiritual issues unlike most psychotherapeutic programs. As a result, we overloaded the schedule with activities in an attempt to provide something for everyone, which led to patient dissatisfaction and staff exhaustion.

Weekly personnel meetings were vexatious, so we introduced in-service training to avoid the complaints. It turned out to be our salvation. Desperate for something new, we examined the genetic and environmental factors in addiction, especially the influence of the family and childhood. We wallowed in the scientific data and explored alternative approaches, from crystals and visualization to "Outbound Challenges." I took the broad view in our efforts to improve our treatment programs and completed a doctoral thesis entitled, "General Systems Theory and the Treatment of Chemical Dependency." It added little. In fact, more analysis brought only more confusion to the treatment program.

[2] We recognize an oxymoron here.

[3] Only five percent of those who join Alcoholics Anonymous remain after one year. See: John Bragg, *Comments On AA's Triennial Survey* (New York: AA General Service Office, 1990). For an exhaustive discussion of this issue join the Addict-L list server: E-mail To: listserv@listserv.kent.edu and "subscribe addict-l" in the body of the message without colons and no subject.

[4] Also called hermeneutics. See A. Parry and R. Doan, *Story Re-Visions: Narrative Therapy in the Postmodern World* (New York: Guilford Press, 1994).

[5] Atheistic self-help groups such as Rational Recovery (http://rational.org/recovery/) are on the increase.

The first light came with a study of Scott Peck's *Road Less Traveled* and *Further Along the Road Less Traveled*. We did not find his introduction of spirituality into psychiatry relevant, but the subtle shift from an analytic to an holistic, from a literal to a poetic, view of mental health was refreshing even though we felt uncomfortable with abandoning analytic psychology for a more humanistic approach. James Hillman's book, *We've Had a Hundred Years of Psychotherapy and the World's Getting Worse*[6] pushed us yet farther, and for the first time we openly questioned the efficacy of psychology or psychiatry to treat addiction. Some of our professionals took umbrage at this move, and we lost them.

With Hillman's *Archetypal Psychology: A Brief Account* as a guide,[7] we launched a long and arduous study of archetypal psychology. To appreciate archetypal psychology "as a cultural movement part of whose task is the re-visioning of psychology, psychopathology, and psychotherapy in terms of the Western cultural imagination"[8] required questioning our fundamental suppositions. Since this approach is designated archetypal "psychology," the tendency was to use the current popular concepts of academic and therapeutic psychology as points of reference. This was frustrating. Not until we realized that we were dealing with an overarching philosophical viewpoint were we able to move forward. Some of our remaining professionals still resisted, so we read and studied the texts as a group, chapter by chapter.

Our early discussions focused on Hillman's use of soul, a study made difficult because we used Thomas Moore's work. Moore's writing was accessible, but it kept returning us to a singular Christian "soul as object." It was difficult for us to grasp soul as "a perspective rather than a substance, a viewpoint toward things rather than a thing itself"[9] and to "try to see soul not as a singular but multiple itself."[10] We still struggle with these ideas and occaisionally need to remind ourselves that this very struggle is soul.

[6] James Hilllman and Michael Ventura, *We've Had a Hundred Years of Psychotherapy and the World's Getting Worse* (San Francisco: HarperSan Francisco, 1992).

[7] I developed a thirty page staff study guide with some highlights of the book, *Archetypal Psychology: A Brief Account*, by James Hillman (Woodstock, Conn.: Spring Publications, 1983; rpt. 1997). A copy, including notes by Hillman, is available on our Website.

[8] James Hillman, *Archetypal Psychology: A Brief Account*, 10.

[9] James Hillman, *Re-Visioning Psychology* (New York: Harper Perennial, 1976), xvi.

[10] Personal correspondence from James Hillman to John Burns, May, 1998.

We also spent time discussing the archetype of addiction, but it was Rafael López-Pedraza who helped us see that compulsive use is not archetypal, but Titanic, "no law, no order, no limits."[11] This saved us from the trap of using the archetype as a type or diagnostic category. However, the real change came when we began to focus on "the poetic basis of mind."[12] Considering chemical dependency treatment from a poetic, intuitive, aesthetic, and holistic bias as opposed to a literal, analytic, scientific or academic bias caused a deep personal and professional shift, a sea change.

When asked to consider treatment from a poetic basis of mind, therapists generally reply that they already do this since the goal of treatment is improved quality of life or renewed spiritual values. Yet, brief examination demonstrates how the Twelve-Steps, especially the first five, are used as instruments to "penetrate denial," evoke "surrender" and "acceptance" of some cause for the addiction. This approach is analytic and literal.

Developing a poetic basis of mind is a lengthy and arduous task and requires a new epistemology which questions the fundamental assumptions of current therapy. Pathology is seen "as existentially human and hence fundamentally normal."[13] It is difficult for some to accept that "each life is formed by its unique image, an image that is the essence of that life and calls it destiny"[14] and to see each image as different, as the totality of the "specific context, mood, and scene."[15] The Golden Rule of this form of therapy is "stick to the image,"[16] which presents rather than represents, connotes rather than denotes, evokes rather than describes.[17] Our therapy attempts to deepen, not change, the image and help a person in treatment to gain perspective and appreciation of this image so that the compulsive use of a psychoactive drug no longer fits the picture.

---

[11] See R. López-Pedraza, *Cultural Anxiety* (Einsiedeln: Daimon Verlag, 1990). See especially chapter one, "Moon Madness—Titanic Love."

[12] James Hillman, *Archetypal Psychology: A Brief Account,* 14.

[13] *Ibid.*, 50.

[14] James Hillman, *The Soul's Code: In Search of Character and Calling* (New York: Random House, 1996), 39.

[15] James Hillman, "An Inquiry into Image," *Spring 1977*, 62.

[16] Attributed to Rafael López-Pedraza. See Patricia Berry, "An Approach to the Dream," *Spring 1974*, 61.

[17] James Hillman, "An Inquiry into Image," *Spring 1977*, 84.

Hillman's helpful move here is one of restoration. "Its therapeutic aim [is] neither social adaptation nor personalistic individualizing but rather a work in service of restoration of the patient to imaginal realities."[18] And images are multiple. "The healthy or mature or ideal personality will thus show cognizance of its dramatically masked and ambiguous situation. Irony, humor, and compassion are its hallmarks, since these traits bespeak an awareness of the multiplicity of meanings and fates and the multiplicity of intentions embodied by any subject at any moment."[19] The goal is no longer growth towards perfection.

For us the principle door to the image is story. We use art, music, sports, and poetry, but the life story related in a gathering of people with a similar experience provides the most economic access to the image. Sometimes we need to be reminded that the story is the fiction of the moment, the necessary illusion and is not the image, but reveals the image.[20] Unfortunately the tendency is to interpret story, destroying both the story and the image. When a story session becomes boring that is generally what is happening.

It was difficult to abandon individual therapy sessions—although they were time consuming, costly, and divisive—until we were directed towards the final chapter of Robert Stein's book, *Incest and Human Love* (re-released recently in its original title *The Betrayal of the Soul in Psychotherapy*). "The use of transference as a therapeutic instrument is bad for the soul,"[21] he says. "The lack of group experience is an unfortunate omission in orthodox analysis."[22] And it was enlightening to be told: "To attempt to tell another how he is experiencing me is a bit of destructive scientific hubris."[23]

Merging archetypal psychology with Twelve-Step treatment has produced a better product and improved results at a lower cost. Highly paid professionals have been replaced by social workers who

[18] James Hillman, *Archetypal Psychology: A Brief Account*, 12.

[19] *Ibid.*, 64.

[20] Why recounting the story in a group setting is so effective is seldom questioned because its impact is obvious, but the most profound and technical explanation can be found in Gregory Bateson's brilliant contribution to the study of alcoholism and AA in his chapter, "The Cybernetics of Self: A Theory of Alcoholism" to be found in his book, *Steps to An Ecology of the Mind*, New York: Ballantine Books, 1972, and in the periodical *Psychiatry*, Vol. 34, No. 1., 1-18.

[21] Robert Stein, *Incest and Human Love* (Dallas: Spring Publications, 1973), 157.

[22] *Ibid.*, 160.

[23] *Ibid.*, 157.

administer a simpler program. In the morning there is a didactic presentation and the telling or re-telling of a personal narrative. In the afternoon there is a "feelings group" followed by diverse common activities such as art, music, or sports. Evenings are free for attending Alcoholics or Narcotics Anonymous meetings. There is adequate free time for the dependents to exchange their stories informally. We have learned to open spaces and trust the patients with each other.

As a business we could claim the product markets well. To present this position to the public we organized aesthetic events such as Shakespeare's *King Lear*, Dante's *Comédia*, *The Myths of Pyche and Eros*, *I Ching*, *The Seven Capital Sins*, fairy tales, Marlowe's *Faust*, dream analysis, popular music, and folk festivals. We viewed them all in light of archetypal psychology. Participants often leave with the feeling that we are doing something different and profound.

Of course, the rate of recovery is the primary indicator of effectiveness. We know that patients who come to us from corporations such as Johnson & Johnson, Caterpillar, Goodyear, Avon, the public transportation system, and the petroleum industry have between a sixty and eighty percent recovery rate measured by improved job performance. We can only track the success of private patients by their attendance at aftercare sessions and self-help meetings. That also averages between sixty and eighty percent. When story is the focus, there is a smooth and natural transition between treatment and aftercare. It should be mentioned that Brazil lends itself to innovative approaches since it is a poetic polytheistic culture[24] free from the threat of litigation, obstructive licensing, and certification, nor do we need to pay obeisance to the ever-present diagnostic manual (*DSM*-4), or managed care.

None of this has been easy. I studied Hillman's published writings, traveled to the United States to attend his lectures, listened to the tapes of the Festival of Archetypal Psychology held at the University of Notre Dame in 1992, read through the *Spring Journal* from 1970 to date, and the relevant works of Adolf Guggenbühl-Craig, Charles Boer, David Miller, Edward Casey, Ginette Paris, Greg Mogenson, Mary Watkins, Rafael López-Pedraza, and Robert Stein. Jay Livernois, C. L. Sebrell, Charles Boer, Ben Sells, and López-Pedraza all patiently

---

[24] See John Burns, "A Twelve Step Meeting of the Afro-Brazilian Gods," *Spring 61*, 1997, 113-124.

led us through long, intense discussions configuring archetypal psychology to the treatment of chemical dependency. Like archetypal psychology itself, this effort has been open-ended, constantly metamorphosing, appearing in different guises and interpretations in each of our centers.

Hillman's summary of the process resonates with the Twelve-Step approach of Alcoholics Anonymous and best expresses the goal of our program:

> There is a further consequence of the credit one pays to the images of the soul. A new feeling of self-forgiveness and self-acceptance begins to spread and circulate. It is as if the heart and the left side were extending their dominion. Shadow aspects of the personality continue to play their burdensome roles but now within a larger tale, the myth of oneself, just what one is which begins to feel as if that is how one is meant to be. My myth becomes my truth; my life symbolic and allegorical. Self-forgiveness, self-acceptance, self-love; more, one finds oneself sinful but not guilty, grateful for the sins one has and not another's, loving one's lot even to the point of desire to have and to be always in this vivid inner connection with one's own individual portion.[25]

[25] James Hillman, *Insearch: Psychology and Religion*, 2nd Revised Edition (Woodstock, Conn.: Spring Publications, 1994), 119.

Will You Be My Mother? An Archetypal Approach to the Healing of Compulsive Overeaters

TRICIA NOLL COLBY

> *Countries like ours are full of people who have all the material comforts they desire, yet live lives of quiet (and at times noisy) desperation, understanding nothing except there is a hole inside of them and that however much food and drink they pour into it, however many motorcars and television sets they stuff it with, however many well balanced children and loyal friends they parade around the edge of it…it aches.* (Ferguson, 1980)

The conditions of being overweight and eating compulsively are rampant in American culture these days. Despite avid attempts at being conscious about health, the problem continues to escalate with no end in sight. In an attempt to master the problem, grocery baskets are filled with low fat entrees and condiments, sugar substitutes and chemical alternatives to food. Numerous dollars are spent on diet programs and health club memberships. Ears are stapled, stomachs and intestines are clamped. Shakes and diet pills are ingested. And while many of these things work on their own, the problem continues. The overeating is but a symptom of a larger issue that is pervasive in American culture, an issue that has yet to be acknowledged or addressed by most people. That is, we as a culture

Tricia Noll Colby is a counselor who resides in San Diego. She received a doctorate in clinical psychology from Pacifica Graduate Institute.

are out of control in many areas of our lives. Addictive behaviors prevail everywhere we go. Nothing is ever enough to assuage the insatiable hunger we experience inside. No amount of money, possessions, food, or drink seems to fill the abyss. The syndrome of compulsive overeating will be expressed here not as a result of poor willpower or a need for physical restraint but as a disease in itself—an addictive disease that has the potential to be deadly; one that can ravish the bodies and souls of those who are afflicted with it. Compulsive overeating is a disease that has its etiology in childhood and is perpetuated by the culture. The prevalence of the disease is a place of entry that the gods have chosen to summon our attention and speak to us about the culture we are living in.

Overeaters Anonymous (1980) stated that obesity is unquestionably one of the major health problems in the United States. In 1980 the numbers of overweight individuals in the United States ranged from ten million to more than seventy million, depending on the criteria used to classify an individual as obese. Since then the number of overweight individuals has steadily increased. Overeaters Anonymous (1980) stated that in 1973 a Gallup Poll revealed that forty-six percent of Americans felt they were overweight. Four or five out of ten Americans were doing something to control their weight. By 1993 (Cooks and Descutner) studies suggested that the number of individuals afflicted with eating disorders was even greater than reported. Now, there is an increase in those afflicted with these disorders with far more women than men suffering from them.

Culturally, women have most often been assigned the roles of tending to the preparation of food and the feeding of the species. And since food is such a part of women's lives, it makes sense that they would be the ones who most often suffer from psychological issues surrounding food. With an obsession with food also comes an obsession with weight and a body size that is defined as acceptable by the culture. According to Sears and Lawren (1995), the average American woman has thirty-two percent body fat, fifty percent fatter than the ideal that is defined by the culture. This is the average American woman. The obese woman who suffers from compulsive overeating is often much larger than this, which poses a problem not only with image but with physical health.

While once considered primarily a condition faced by adults, obesity has now filtrated down to our children. On a recent episode of the *Today Show*, it was stated that one out of four children suffers from some form of overeating and weight problem. In 1980, medical doctor William Rader stated in *Overeaters Anonymous* that compulsive overeating was a serious disease that was devastating this country. The devastation has only escalated since then with our children becoming the newest victims.

The first step of the Twelve-Steps of Overeaters Anonymous states that the compulsive overeater is powerless over food and her life is unmanageable. While all people who are overweight are not compulsive overeaters, it does appear that society's obsessions with body size, image, fats, carbohydrates, excessive exercising, and dieting are, in fact, out of control. This is a frightening thought. There are huge numbers of people in our culture unable to manage their lives. And this is only one form of addictive disease. Put them all together without a remedy, and we are a culture in trouble.

Redefining the Problem

According to Post (1993) compulsive overeating is defined as a condition characterized by binge eating and/or continuous eating, without regard to physiological cues. A condition where food is used as a means to cope, to comfort, or to restore physical, emotional, and spiritual states to a previous sense of equilibrium. While both men and women are afflicted, this article will focus on the disease of compulsive overeating in women for the reasons stated above.

Developing a solution to a problem rests first in defining it. If the problem with compulsive overeating is only seen as physical, then the solution will be sought through manipulating the body in such a manner to create change. But if one defines the problem as encompassing a broader cultural basis, then the solution can be sought from a much different realm. The ingestion of large amounts of food is not in order to satisfy a physical need but a spiritual one. Deep in the soul rests an emptiness. There is not enough food, drink, or material things to fill it, and so the soul hungers and aches. From an archetypal perspective, this hunger can be imagined as the presence of the negative pole of the Great Mother in all of her grandeur. The solution may rest in the repair of this archetype, and no gym or diet pill can accomplish this. It can only be achieved through a corrective experience of loving relatedness to others.

One primary arena available to the compulsive overeater today for the healing of the archetype of the Great Mother is the fellowship of Overeaters Anonymous. During meetings, compulsive overeaters have opportunities to experience the relatedness they may need to heal the negative pole of the archetype. The compulsive overeater's relationship with food is balanced with the experience of the positive pole of the archetype expressed through close loving relationships with others in the community.

By viewing compulsive overeating and food addiction as a disease, one can look at it through different eyes. No longer is it viewed as just a condition where one suffers from a weakness. Instead it can be seen as a dis-ease in the balance of body and soul. The disharmony is a call which, if heard, offers an opportunity to achieve wholeness. Diets, pills, or exercise plans alone cannot create the balance needed to treat this disease. The soul is crying out to be filled not deprived or abused.

Food addiction may be one of the most difficult diseases of addiction to treat. Rather than being able to refrain from the substances they are addicted to, those people addicted to food must continue to ingest it to live. The three most common disorders of food addiction are anorexia nervosa, bulimia, and compulsive overeating. Those afflicted with anorexia nervosa starve their bodies to death. Bulimics take in enormous amounts of food and then regurgitate or purge it. This also depletes their bodies of the necessary nutrients to live. Compulsive overeaters take in large amounts of food, and it remains in their bodies. Their bodies are abused by the increased chemicals from the food they eat which is deposited in the boldily systems. No matter which manifestation the disease of food addiction takes, the result is much pain and suffering for the individual. Ziegler (1983) said this pain results from excesses, from damage to the body exceeding normal wear and tear which sets in where the contact of blow, bite, break, or cut was destructive. It comes from excessive stretching or straining within the body. For those experiencing the disease of food addiction, the body is in a continual state of physical unbalance and pain. Whether it is being abused by being depleted of nutritional substances, as is the case with the anorexic or bulimic, or is being intoxicated with them by the compulsive overeater, the result is the same.

Modern medical science views disease as something to arrest, to be rid of. This is not how disease has been viewed in the past. The Greeks believed that sickness was the result of divine intervention, that something profound was being asked by the divine powers (Reis, 1991). The god or goddess was thought to be both the cause and the cure for illness. Jung (1962) echoed this belief when he said, "The gods have become diseases." According to Jung, we are so alienated from the sacred dimension of life that divine energy, in desperation, has chosen our bodies as a place of entry. Modern people have become so alienated from their souls that the only way the divine can enter their consciousness is through the body in the form of disease.

Any disease carries with it pain and suffering. And it is through pain and suffering that we often rise to higher levels of consciousness and experience deeper levels of meaning. Religious leaders have been professing the benefits of pain and suffering from ages past to the present. St. John of the Cross wrote about the spiritual blessings infused by God into the soul through suffering and pain. He said the process of illumination and receiving the outpouring of God's love plunges man into darkness and causes him affliction and distress. Man then is enkindled with passionate, yet afflictive love until he is spiritualized and refined. Later thinkers also wrote on this subject, identifying suffering as a call to a spiritual awakening.

> One can activate value on a spiritual level only in confrontations with unavoidable suffering, where there is no way out except through the darkest center of a painful experience. One has no choice whether to face this suffering or not, but just because of the fierce limitation, one great possibility does remain--of choosing how one will react to the unavoidable suffering. This choice of attitude may activate our spiritual values, defining and asserting what has supreme importance, what will stand when everything else crumbles (Frankl, 1965, 64-65).

Those suffering from addictive diseases also experience a great deal of pain and suffering. It is this pain and suffering which often brings them in the doors of Overeaters Anonymous. In such programs the progress of recovery requires that they begin to see their suffering as a call from the gods to wake up and become conscious. One could say that their recovery begins with the divine suffering of St. John of the Cross—along with the light comes the darkness. In the terms of archetypal psychology, they descend to the Underworld where the spiritual awakening begins to unfold, piece by piece. All the while they are being supported by the members of the fellowship.

The Wounds

The disease of compulsive overeating may have its origins in childhood. Often it can be seen that this addiction comes as a direct result of the wounding of the maternal archetype. Because this archetype is carried by the earthly mother, that relationship is of primary importance in the molding of the child. When an injury occurs in the normal development of the maternal archetype in childhood, the psyche is impeded from developing out of a childlike state into adulthood (Harding, 1993). When this archetype is not constellated in childhood, the phase of ego consciousness remains childlike, that is, dependent, as is a child, in relationship to the unconscious (Newman, 1956). It is not so much that the mother archetype is obliterated but that it has not been activated by human experience. And having never been activated, it remains in the unconscious, latent, not even appearing as an image (Harding, 1993, 16).

More often than not, the mothers of compulsive overeaters have not received adequate mothering themselves. Without having had their own maternal archetype constellated, they are unable to impart this to their children. As a result, a particular pattern of mothering is carried down from one generation to the next. This can often be observed by a compulsive overeater who has identified her disease and then begins to track backwards through the generations of women before who have all appeared to have been suffering from the same symptoms. Often the women in past generations were not aware of their conditions. Perhaps they just considered themselves fat or the victim of a genetic predisposition or glandular disorder that caused their bodies to be misshapened.

This familial trend is a huge problem, especially for women. Most people in this generation, male and female, do not have a strong maternal matrix out of which to go forward into life (Woodman, 1982, 16). A mother whose maternal archetype remains unconscious and inactivated cannot mother either herself or her child adequately. As infants, when her child cries to have its instinctual needs met, the mother attempts to sooth the child with food. Because of her own inadequacies, she knows not what else to offer. This kind of behavior on the part of the mother leads to the child experiencing the confusing of instincts from early infancy on. Every physiological state gets responded to through the giving of food. The natural mother answers the child's instinctual cries with food out of her own inner lack of resources to meet them in other ways (Woodman, 1980, 95). The pattern of response that develops in the child—whenever she feels a physiological discomfort, she reaches for food to relieve it. This then begins to generalize into whatever feeling is experienced. Positive or negative, feelings are responded to with food. Thus, a pattern of continuous eating develops in response to life's experiences.

One would think that without the maternal archetype being constellated, that the mother would not be in touch with either the negative or positive poles of the archetype. However, this often does not appear to be the case. Many compulsive overeaters have been under the sway of a mother who primarily operates out of the negative pole of this archetype. Overeaters rarely report having experienced the unconditional love and nurturing from their mothers. Instead they have experienced feeling poisoned, smothered, devoured and criticized by their mothers. Instead of feeling they were provided with positive, life-giving experiences that would nurture the development of their psyches, they feel they were torn down and destroyed while they were still in the process of being molded.

The soul may rest underneath, but because of the fragmentation of the pieces of the psyche, overeaters are unable to access it. Seeking perfection as opposed to destruction, they devour huge amounts of food which poison their bodies. The moments of satisfaction after such behavior are momentary. Soon they are aware of feeling intoxicated and guilty. Then they berate themselves for their failure to make good choices. Out of balance in body and soul and feeling bad, they begin the process all over again in an attempt to soothe their unrest by ingesting more food. Inside they know that the food is not the answer, but they ache, and the only proven method of momentarily alleviating the pain has been through the devouring of more food. Having no other model but the negative mother to relate to, they are caught in a cycle of destruction. Psychic growth and development are frozen. There seems to be no way out of the cycle. Feeling isolated and alone, they long for attachment and community with others. But this attchment is unattainable because they feel different and unworthy as if they were damaged merchandise. They feel that the world only sees the fat on their bones not the sadness in their souls. Many of these women will die psychic deaths if a solution is not found in time. The healing lies in being able to disengage from this negative pole of the archetype and having a new experience with the positive pole of the archetype through a relatedness to others. One must find a place where they can be re-parented by a family in which the maternal archetype is present in its positive aspect. It is through this process that the wounds can be healed.

Old and New Relationships

When the compulsive overeaters first walk in to the doors of Overeaters Anonymous, they are living a life of isolation. Their lives are void of interpersonal relationships. The most important relationship to them is between them and their food. While they may be part of a family, a social group or a member of a church or synagogue, all those relationships are subservient to their relationship with food. To heal, the compulsive overeater must replace the relationship with food with loving relationships with others.

Scholars and theologians have been talking about the healing power of relationships for centuries. One need only pick up the *New Testament* and read some of the many parables of Jesus to understand the healing power of relatedness. Contemporary writing also highlights this power. "From the most advanced scholarship in fields of biophysics to botany, archaeology to cell science, sociology to neurophysiology, we are learning that we belong to one another and are sustained by one another"(Anderson and Hopkins, 1991, 178). Compulsive overeaters do not get the sustenance they need for their emotional and spiritual needs when their primary relationship is with the inanimate substance of food. The fellowship of Overeaters Anonymous provides a setting where compulsive overeaters can begin to experience relatedness to others in a manner different from the way that has been experienced in the past. As a result, over time, compulsive overeaters become able to disengage from the negative, outmoded archetypes that their parents carried.

While relating to others in fellowship is a salient feature of the program, the concept of relating to a higher power is paramount to the Overeaters Anonymous program. From an archetypal perspective, this higher power carries all the qualities of the positive pole of the

Great Mother archetype. The unconditional love and positive mothering they missed as a child is experienced by establishing a relationship with a higher power. This relationship allows compulsive overeaters to experience a reprieve from the devouring, possessive, and judgmental experience of the negative pole of this archetype as it expresses itself in society and in their disease. For many this higher power becomes the Christian God. This concept brings with it all the past associations they had with God. Often the patriarchal God has been the image they carried and projected onto other men in their lives. Instead of a judgmental God who condemns and is to be feared, they are able to experience through these fellowships a new, more feminine image of God, a God who nurtures and supports them instead of condemns or judges, one who answers their pleas for help. By honoring what is personally true for them rather than old messages that tell them what they ought to be, they are able to heal. This new avenue for connection with the divine is often constructed and validated by the other group members. In time, the group becomes a vessel of transmission for divine or sacred forces. A *temenos* is created, the sacred vessel, the safe place where they can go and not be judged.

Archetypal Healing

The healing that occurs in the Twelve-Step fellowships is no less than an enactment of the archetype of rebirth. Broken people drag themselves into the doors of the fellowship. Often, they have tried everything else and failed. In many respects their lives are in shambles. They cannot seem to get control over any of their affairs. As they participate, doing what others have done before them, they begin to transform. They begin to come alive again. Perhaps they feel alive for the first time. The experience of the transcendence of life is experienced through the experiences of becoming initiated into the fellowship and partaking in the sacred rituals of the program. According to Jung, the experience of an initiate who takes part in a sacred rite reveals the continuum of life through transformation and renewal. "In these mystery-dramas the transcendence of life, as distinct from its momentary concrete manifestations, is usually represented by the fateful transformations—death and rebirth—of a god or godlike hero." (Jung, 1969, 51)

For many years the members of the fellowship talk about how the god that ruled their life was food. The healing does not come easily, and if an overeater stops attending the fellowship, the symptoms often return. Jung understood that while the group does produce a change in the individual, it will not last. The group can give the individual courage, a bearing, and dignity, but this effect often does not continue once the overeater leaves the group and goes back to everyday life. Therefore, it is necessary to have continual exposure to mass intoxication in order to consolidate the experience and belief in it. (Jung, 1969, 60). A frequently used statement in the Overeater Anonymous fellowship is to keep coming back until the miracle happens.

Works Cited

Anderson, S. and Hopkins, P. *The Feminine Face of God: The Unfolding of the Sacred in Women.* New York: Bantam Books, 1991.

Cooks, L. and Descutner, D. "Different Paths from Powerlessness to Empowerment: A Dramatistic Analysis of Two Eating Disorder Therapies," *Western Journal of Communication*, 57 Fall 1993, 494-514.

Ferguson, M. *The Aquarian Conspiracy.* Los Angeles: J. P. Tarcher, 1980.

Frankl, V. *The Doctor and the Soul: From Psychotherapy to Logotherapy.* Trans. Richard and Clara Winston. New York: Alfred A. Knopf, 1965.

Harding, E. *The Parental Image: Its Injury and Reconstruction.* Boston: Sigo Press, 1993.

Jung, C. G. *Four Archetypes.* Princeton: Princeton UP, 1969.

_________. *The Secret of the Golden Flower.* Trans. Richard Wilhelm. London: Routledge & Kegan Paul, 1962.

Neuman, E. "The Moon and Matriarchal Consciousness," *Spring* 1956.

The New Oxford Annotated Bible with the Apocrypha. Edited by H. May and B. Metzer. New York: Oxford UP, 1977.

Overeaters Anonymous, Inc. *Overeaters Anonymous.* Torrance, Calif., 1980.

Post, G. "Who is the Compulsive Overeater?" *Perspective.* Winter, 4, 1993.

Reis, P. *Through the Goddess: Woman's Way of Healing.* New York: Continuum, 1991.

Sears, B. (with Lawren, B.). *The Zone.* New York: Harper Collins, 1995.

St. John of the Cross. *Dark Night of the Soul.* Ed. and trans. by E. Allison Peers. New York: Doubleday, 1990.

Ulanov, A. *The Feminine in Jungian Psychology and in Christian Theology.* Evanston, Ill.: Northwestern UP, 1971.

Woodman, M. *Addicted to Perfection.* Toronto, Canada: Inner City Books, 1982.

___________. *The Owl Was a Baker's Daughter: Obesity, Anorexia Nervosa and the Repressed Feminine.*Toronto: Inner City Books, 1980.

Ziegler, A. *Archetypal Medicine.* Trans. Gary Hartman. Dallas: Spring, 1983.

TISSOT AND *L'ONANISME*: A SHADOW IN THE ENLIGHTENMENT

PATRICK SINGY

Tout est bien sortant des mains de l'auteur des choses, tout dégénére entre les mains de l'homme.[1] —Rousseau, *Emile*

L. D****, watchmaker, had been well-behaved, and had enjoyed a good state of health, until the age of seventeen, when he gave himself up to masturbation, which he repeated every day, often up to three times, and ejaculation was always preceded and accompanied by a mild loss of consciousness, and by a convulsive movement in the extensor muscles of the head, tossing the head strongly back, during which time the neck swelled extraordinarily. A year had not passed before he began to feel a remarkable decay of strength after each act; this notification was not sufficient to lead him out of the quagmire; his soul had already given itself entirely over to this filth and was incapable of forming any other idea, and so he repeated his crime more frequently than before, until he reached the point of being afraid for his life. Because he had too late grown wise, the harm had already made such progress, that he could not be cured

[1] "All is well when it leaves the hands of the author of things, all degenerates in the hands of man." First words of Rousseau's first book, *Emile*, 245. Unless otherwise noted, translations throughout the text are my own.

Patrick Singy was born in Geneva, Switzerland, and he studied psychology at the University of Geneva. He is now a graduate student in the history and philosophy of science at the University of Chicago.

anymore; and the private parts had become so irritable and so weak that this unfortunate did not need to act in order for the semen to pour out. The slightest irritation resulted right away in an imperfect erection that was followed immediately with an evacuation of semen, which daily increased his weakness. This spasm, which before he had felt only during the act, and which had stopped in the same time, had now become usual and often attacked him without any apparent cause, and with such violence, that during the time of the fit, which sometimes lasted fifteen hours, and never less than eight, he felt such violent pains in the hinder part of the neck, that usually he did not scream but howled; it was impossible for him, while the fit lasted, to swallow anything, liquid or solid. His voice had become hoarse, but I did not notice that it was worse during the act. He totally lost his strength; forced to give up his occupation, incapable of everything, overwhelmed with misery, he languished for some months almost without assistance; and what made him the more to be pitied is that he kept some remains of memory—that soon disappeared—which only served constantly to recall to him the causes of his wretchedness and to increase the horror of remorse. I was told of his condition and I went to him; I found what was less a living human being than a corpse lying upon a straw, meager, pale, sallow, sending forth an infectious smell, and almost incapable of any motion. He bled at the nose a pale and aqueous blood, and was continually foaming at the mouth; attacked with diarrhea, his excrements came from him in his bed without his perceiving; the flow of semen was continual; his eyes were rheumy, cloudy, dulled and could not move anymore; his pulse was extremely weak, fast and frequent; he had breathing difficulties, he was excessively skinny, except as regards his feet, which began to become oedematous. The disorder of his mind was not less than that of his body; without ideas, without memory, unable to link two sentences, without reflection, without being afraid of his fate, without any other sensation but that of a pain which returned with every fit, at least once in three days. A human being far below a beast; a sight of which one is unable to conceive the horror, it was difficult to admit that he belonged to mankind in the past. With fortifying medicines, I quickly succeeded in destroying those violent spasmodic fits that reminded him so cruelly that he was still alive only through pain; being satisfied with having mitigated his tortures, I discontinued remedies, which could have no efficacy on the main of his disorder; he died at the end of a few weeks, in June, 1757, oedamatous throughout his body.[2]

[2] Tissot, *L'Onanisme*, 44-46. Here I use the most recent French edition.

This quotation is a representative extract of *L'Onanisme*, a book written by Samuel-Auguste-André-David Tissot in 1760. Between 1760 and 1886, there were at least sixty-three editions of *L'Onanisme, Dissertation Physique sur les Maladies Produites par la Masturbation*, and thirty-four translations in five languages.[3] *L'Onanisme* became a reference book among the most famous physicians of the eighteenth century as well as among the *philosophes*, and Louis François Luc de Lignac (1740-1809) even spoke of the "revolution" made by *L'Onanisme*.[4] The nature of this revolution lies in the content of the book: it was the first devoted to this topic from a purely medical viewpoint without religious argument. Therefore, to focus on Tissot is to illustrate an important change that occurred during the Enlightenment: the transfer of power, from Church to medicine, from religion to science—the "secularization and medicalization of morality."[5]

Tissot was born on March 20, 1728 in the village of Grancy, near Lausanne, Switzerland. His family was Protestant and "belonged to the educated professional segment of the rural population."[6] At seventeen he decided to go to Montpellier to study medicine. He received his degree in 1749 and left Montpellier to return to his Calvinist *Pays de Vaud*. His first book, *L'Inoculation Justifiée*, published in 1754, was a success. It was also a victory over the religious prejudice of the time, traditional medicine, and superstitious people who condemned the practice of inoculation. The first edition of *L'Onanisme* appeared in Latin in 1758, followed two years later by an expanded French version.

Tissot afterwards wrote several other medical books that became best sellers, such as *Avis au Peuple sur sa Santé* (1761), which brought him notoriety. Tissot's success was partly responsible for attracting wealthy foreigners to Lausanne and for contributing to make famous the outskirts of this city.[7] Tissot died on June 13, 1797, after having participated in the reformation of medical studies, notably by publishing in 1785 his *Essai sur les Moyens de Perfectionner les Études de Médecine*.[8]

---

[3] Tarczylo, *Sexe et liberté au siècle des Lumières*, 114.

[4] De Lignac, *A Physical View of Man and Woman in a State of Marriage*, xxi.

[5] Rosario, "Phantastical Pollutions: the Public Threat of Private Vice in France," in *Solitary Pleasures*, 103-104.

[6] Emch-Dériaz, *Tissot: Physician of the Enlightenment*, 10.

[7] Stengers and van Neck, *Histoire d'une grande peur, la masturbation*, 74-75.

[8] A useful bibliography on Tissot can be found in a booklet published on the occasion of the symposium on "La médecine des Lumières: autour de S.A.A.D Tissot," that was held in Lausanne between October 9 and 11, 1997.

The Cultural Onus Against Masturbation

The religious argument in Europe against masturbation is traceable back to the ancient Hebrews.[9] During the Middle Ages monks still condemned masturbation, but the penance could vary a great deal depending on the monastery. Some required two years of penance, while others declared masturbation a mortal sin.[10] In any case, it was considered a serious sin. However, after Jean Gerson's (1363-1429) *De Confessione Mollitiei* (*On the Confession of Masturbation*), in the fifteenth century, there was no known book to explain how to unmask the masturbator, as if the clergy had lost interest in the subject.[11]

If one wants to find the very beginning of medical discourse against masturbation, one will not turn to Tissot. The first physicians who claimed that masturbation was dangerous to health belonged to the second half of the seventeenth century. Jean Stengers and Anne Van Neck found two such physicians whose books offered only some brief allusions to the consequences of masturbation: impotence and gonorrhea.[12] More important is an anonymous book published in London around 1715: *Onania, or the Heinous Sin of Self-Pollution, and All its Frightful Consequences, in Both Sexes, Consider'd, with Spiritual and Physical Advice to Those, who have Already Injur'd Themselves by this Abominable Practice*. Here, for the first time, masturbation was described as a cause of death. Many young men, the author said, were "sent to their graves" because of this vice.[13] But as the title indicates, this book maintains a religious argument, in addition to the rather new medical one, with the author quoting on the first page a passage from the *Bible* where God kills Onan because the latter did not want to fulfill his duty to his dead brother's wife by producing offspring for his brother and instead "spilled his semen on the ground."[14]

---

[9] Bullough, *Sexual Variance in Society and History*, 74-89.

[10] *Ibid.*, 358. See also Stengers and van Neck, *Histoire d'une grande peur*, 29.

[11] Stengers and van Neck, *Histoire d'une grande peur*, 29-35.

[12] *Ibid.*, 43-44.

[13] Anonymous, *Onania*, 18.

[14] *Genesis* 38: 8-10. This passage led to two different interpretations (Onan masturbated or Onan practiced *coitus interruptus*), and to two different definitions of the word "onanism," which referred for a long time either to masturbation (in the secular vocabulary) or to *coitus interruptus* (in the specialized theological literature). See Stengers and van Neck, *Histoire d'une grande peur*, 206. In *Onania* as well as in *L'Onanisme*, the issue is about masturbation, not about *coitus interruptus.*

Therefore, if some allusions were made or articles written on masturbation from a medical viewpoint prior to Tissot, they are not to be found in a medical book exclusively dedicated to the topic.[15] This relative silence on the part of medicine is not surprising. According to the Galenic medical theory which was still influential in the eighteenth century, it was maintained that it could be dangerous to hold the sperm too long. If Galen (c.130-c.200 C.E.), in his work, did not explicitly draw the conclusion that masturbation was a healthy practice, he nevertheless spoke about Diogenes (c.404-c.323 B.C.E.), whose health seemed to be linked with his practice of masturbation.[16] But for Galen, sperm was also a precious humor, so it could be dangerous to scatter it too much. Tissot agreed almost completely with Galen's theory, even on the fact that sometimes an ejaculation without copulation could be healthy. But the new arguments he added transformed the Galenic theory in such a way that it gave masturbation its specificity in making its consequences different from the ones of copulation.

Tissot's innovation appears already at first sight to be strongly influenced by religion, for, although traditional medicine declared that sperm was precious, it did not say anything special against masturbation except that sometimes it could be healthy. Tissot's prejudices against masturbation came from the religious realm not from the medical tradition. But he used this medical tradition and leaned on it in order to build his own arguments specifically directed against masturbation. And Tissot was himself aware that he was one of the first physicians to talk about masturbation in public, as he wrote to Jean-Jacques Rousseau (1712-1778): "*L'Onanisme* will prove to you that at last there has been a physician who saw all the danger of this odious practice that you have fought so strongly, and who had the courage to make it known."[17]

---

[15] For a list of some texts on masturbation of the eighteenth century, see Tarczylo, *Sexe et liberté*, 281-288.

[16] Galen, *De locis affectis, book 6*, in *Claudii Galeni Opera Omnia, K VIII*, ed. by C. G. Kuehn, 417-418. See also Stengers and van Neck, *Histoire d'une grande peur*, 41.

[17] Tissot to Rousseau, letter dated 8 July 1762, in *Correspondance complète de Jean-Jacques Rousseau,* Tome XI, juin-juillet 1762, letter number 1966, 239.

Tissot's Argument

In his fight against masturbation, Tissot marked the solemn entrance of a discourse of facts, of proofs, of arguments; onanism had been a mortal sin, but thanks to Tissot, it became a mortal disease. Exit religion, enter science.

According to Tissot, the "seminal liquor" was the most precious of all humors. It was considered much more precious than a wet-nurse's milk and forty times more precious than blood. Tissot had three different proofs for this point which he used as the foundation of his argument. First, "physicians of all centuries"[18] believed that semen was extremely precious. Tissot cites the names of physicians or philosophers from Antiquity—Hippocrates (c.460-c.377 B.C.E.), Galen, and Epicurus (341-270 B.C.E.)—and some physicians of his own era— Hermann Boerhaave (1668-1738) and Friedrich Hoffmann (1660-1742). However, Tissot did not make explicit the difference between the contemporary physicians and ancients, which consists in the fact that the ancients never directly argued against masturbation, rather only against "the abuse of the pleasures of love."[19] Second,

> one can have an idea of [the importance of semen], by observing the effects it produces as soon as it begins to be formed: the voice, the physiognomy, even the features of the face change, beard appears, [etc. Moreover,] true observations prove that amputation of testicles, in the virile age, brought the loss of beard and the return of an infantile voice.[20]

And third, "the weakness felt by those who lose [semen] during the carnal union"[21] proves the importance of this semen.

Tissot further describes semen as an "essential oil," an "active liquor," and its "squandering lets other humors weaken, and, in a certain sense, be evaporated."[22]

> Our bodies suffer a continual waste, and if we could not compensate for what we have lost, we would soon fall into a mortal weakness. This compensation is done with aliments,

[18] Tissot, *L'Onanisme*, 23.
[19] *Ibid.*, 27.
[20] *Ibid.*, 23.
[21] *Ibid.*, 71.
[22] *Ibid.*, 75.

> but those aliments must go through different preparations in our body, that one calls nutrition... Such is the structure (fabrique) of our machine, and of animal machines in general, that, in order that aliments acquire the degree of preparation necessary for repairing the body, there must remain a certain quantity of humors already worked on... If this condition is lacking, digestion and concoction of aliments stays imperfect, and all the more imperfect, that the missing humor happens to be of a more elaborated kind, and of a greater importance.[23]

Tissot asks a rhetorical question in order to prove his point: how can this humor have an effect on the body, since it is contained in "reservoirs," and does not circulate? The answer is given by comparing semen with urine, another humor according to Tissot. Everybody must urinate, yet there are men who never ejaculate. Semen, therefore, is not contained in reservoirs "in order to be, at least entirely, evacuated, but in order to acquire, in those reservoirs, a perfection that makes it appropriate for new functions, when it enters the mass of humors."[24] Appearance of beard and change of voice in men is not a result of getting older, but of the fact that semen is "continually pumped again and mixed again with humors," and that it makes the body work well. This point is proven by the fact that age does not bring on these changes in some animals and in eunuchs, who do not have this precious liquor.[25]

Up to this point, Tissot still relies on other physicians and does not show why masturbation is more dangerous than coitus. His answer to this crucial question appears in the second part of his argument:

> If the dangerous consequences of a too plentiful loss of this humor depended only on the quantity...it would not much matter, in relation to the domain of the body, that this evacuation is done in one or the other ways I indicated [copulation, masturbation, pollution or diseases]... A too plentiful quantity of semen lost according to the ways of nature (*dans les voies de la nature*) throws in detrimental harms, but the latter are much worse when the quantity has been scattered by unnatural means.[26]

[23] *Ibid.*, 22.
[24] *Ibid.*, 76.
[25] *Ibid.*, 78.
[26] *Ibid.*, 24.

Tissot is here employing a qualitative notion, nature, in order to distinguish between the consequences of masturbation and copulation. Since he wants to speak as a physician, he has to prove empirically that unnatural means are more dangerous than natural ones. He gives eight proofs, in which for the most part he does not rely on any other physician. For example, Tissot argues there is an opposition between imagination and nature: masturbation is a dangerous practice because it is stimulated by the imagination, and not by nature.[27] Thus, masturbation has "no obstacle and no limits,"[28] because the imagination itself has no limits. Actually, *L'Onanisme* is more a book on the dangers of excess than on masturbation.[29] Likewise, Rousseau's "*dangereux supplément*" or "*funeste avantage*"[30] is illustrative of this practice which easily leads to "excess" because it relies mainly on imagination. Nature, on the other hand, "inspires desires only when seminal vesicles are filled with a quantity of liquor that has acquired a degree of thickening which makes its reabsorption more difficult; and this shows that its evacuation will not perceptibly weaken the body."[31] A natural evacuation is one that depends on "the quantity of matters to evacuate."[32] This is the reason why, for instance, a nocturnal emission that comes from an "overabundance of semen" is "not an illness, but rather a favorable crisis."[33] This shows that the qualitative distinction between what is natural and what is unnatural can be in fact reduced to a quantitative aspect, which enables Tissot to maintain his logical argument.

Tissot also argues that people, during natural or unnatural sexual acts, perspire a lot and therefore lose a lot of bodily substance; but, during the natural act, one "breathes in what the other exhales," while

[27] *Ibid.*, 94-95.

[28] *Ibid.*, 95.

[29] Mainil, *Dans les règles du plaisir...*, 198-199.

[30] Rousseau, *Les confessions*, Paris, 109. Rousseau and Tissot knew each other. Rousseau read and liked *L'Onanisme*, while Tissot quoted a passage of *Emile* in *L'Onanisme.* Their correspondence has been published in *Annales de la Société Jean-Jacques Rousseau*, tome septième, 19-40. In his *Discours sur l'origine et les fondements de l'inégalité parmi les hommes*, Rousseau describes a man of nature without imagination. The latter appears precisely when the man goes out of the state of nature. Rousseau, *Discours*, 144; see also Starobinski, *L'Œil vivant*, 131-136.

[31] Tissot, *L'Onanisme*, 94.

[32] *Ibid.*

[33] *Ibid.*, 174.

the one who masturbates "loses, but recovers nothing."[34] Tissot's tendency to put everything on a physiological level is exemplified by his argument that "the joy of the soul (*la joie qui tient à l'âme*)"—which is not the bodily pleasure common to human beings and animals—"aids digestion, livens up circulation, encourages all the functions, restores strength and supports it." And because the joy is stronger when the woman is beautiful, Tissot asserts that "the union with a beautiful woman exhausts less than with an ugly one."[35]

Tissot's theory concerns also women's masturbation, which is basically the same as for men because women also lose a humor when they masturbate. This humor is perceived by Tissot as less precious than men's, so one could believe that it is less dangerous to lose it. But since women are assumed to be weaker than men, the terrible consequences of masturbation are the same.[36]

What is important about Tissot's theory are not the details of his arguments but that it never explicitly depends on religious concepts:

> I would like to have recourse to miraculous causes only when we find an obvious contradiction with physical causes. But it is not the case here [with masturbation]: we can explain everything by the laws of mechanism of the body, or by those of its union with soul.[37]

On the other hand, it is evident that Tissot's quantitative and qualitative concept of nature reveals an implicit religious side in *L'Onanisme*. This merging concept is crucial, for the reconciliation of science and religion is made by it precisely because of its possible double connotation. Within the single word "nature," Tissot was able simultaneously to have a medical discourse with its quantitative side and a religious and moral discourse with its qualitative side. In spite of all his

---

[34] *Ibid.*, 101-102.

[35] *Ibid.*, 102-103.

[36] *Ibid.*, 91. For Tissot, the model remains men, women being only a variation of this model. Consecutively, women seem to have suffered less from *L'Onanisme*: in the letters to Tissot, patients who wrote to complain about the troubles due to masturbation were all men. The letters to Tissot written by his patients are at the Bibliothèque Cantonale et Universitaire, Lausanne, Switzerland, in the manuscripts fond IS 3784. Micheline Louis-Courvoisier and Séverine Pilloud are working on these letters at the Institut d'Histoire de la Médecine of the University of Lausanne, constructing an interesting and useful database; I thank them for having allowed me to use this database, although it was not finished.

[37] *Ibid.*, 93.

physiological arguments, when Tissot used the word "nature," he related it to God.[38] Religion did not stand outside of medicine, but, rather, it embraced it:

> This habit to have recourse to supernatural causes was already fought by Hippocrates who, while talking about a disease that Scythians put down to a peculiar punishment of God, had this fine thought: *It is true that this disease comes from God, but they all come from Him; none comes from Him more than another, because all are the result of natural laws that govern everything.*[39]

Moreover, a quick look at the vocabulary used by Tissot and at many more or less implicit allusions in his book can do nothing but convince the reader of the influence of religion on his logical and empirical arguments. Masturbators were "guilty of a crime that the divine justice did not want to postpone the punishment, and that it punishes at once with death."[40] Perhaps in order to avoid a too frequent repetition of the word "masturbation," Tissot used a range of synonyms, like "crime,"[41] "infamy," "abomination," "odious and criminal habit," and "sin." Tissot also implored God's blessing for his work.[42] One can guess that when he referred to masturbation as an "unnatural means"[43] to scatter semen, he had in mind both physiological and religious beliefs.[44] Thus, these two domains—science and religion—are not clearly separated, and this makes possible a moral discourse against masturbation within a medical book. To say, like Teysseire and Verry-Jolivet, that Tissot made masturbation an illness rather than a form of a deviance,[45] is in my opinion doubly wrong. First, and this is a mistake that other authors make,[46] according to Tissot masturbation

[38] God was also defined as "the Author of nature." Tissot, *De la santé des gens de lettres*, 142.

[39] Tissot, *L'Onanisme*, 93.

[40] *Ibid.*, 103.

[41] Although he said he would not write about it: "I will write about the diseases due to masturbation and not about the crime of masturbation." *Ibid.*, 17.

[42] *Ibid.*, 21.

[43] *Ibid.*, 24.

[44] To say, like Tarczylo, that in *L'Onanisme* the sin is not against God, but against nature, is to forget the divine essence of nature. Cf. Tarczylo, "Prêtons la main à la nature: l'onanisme de Tissot," in *Dix-Huitième siècle*, 12, 85.

[45] Teysseire and Verry-Jolivet, "Présentation" to *Avis au peuple sur sa Santé* by Tissot, 10.

[46] Tarczylo and Emch-Dériaz notably.

is not an illness. It is a cause of many illnesses. Second, the vocabulary used by Tissot is imbued with moral connotations. And in fact it is precisely because masturbation is not an illness that it can be morally condemned, for one can blame someone for behavior, but not for illness. Today we blame someone for smoking, not for cancer; Tissot blamed his patients for masturbating, not for dying. But did the readers of the eighteenth century see the religious and moral side of *L'Onanisme*? It seems that the answer is "no."

The Role of Confession in L'Onanisme

It is certainly true that the Catholic Church did not directly contribute to the success of *L'Onanisme*, although it was also against masturbation.[47] Nevertheless, one can wonder if it is not the Church that acted as a catalyst for the takeover of medicine on this issue.

What sets masturbation apart from other sexual activities is that it is, most often, a secret and solitary practice. It is a "corruption...working in the shadows of mystery."[48] If one wants to fight against it, one will first have to find a way to bring it out in the open. Such was the role of the Church which widened "the scope of the confession (*aveu*)."[49] If, with the new medical discourse on sexuality possibly initiated with Tissot, "the essential point is that sex was not only a matter of sensation and pleasure, of law and taboo, but also of truth and falsehood." This new dimension of this discourse was an extension of what "became one of the West's most highly valued techniques for producing truth,"[50] namely confession. Jean Delumeau points out the importance of confession in our society: "between the 'know thyself' of Socrates and the one of Freud, there has been, as a link and multiplier, the huge contribution—the adjective is not too strong—of confession as it was taught and experienced in Catholicism."[51] Foucault further illustrates the point with

> the metamorphosis in literature: we have passed from a pleasure to be recounted and heard, centering on the heroic or marvelous narration of «trials» of bravery or sainthood, to

[47] Stengers and van Neck, *Histoire d'une grande peur*, 103.

[48] Tissot, *L'Onanisme*, 19.

[49] Foucault, *The History of Sexuality: An Introduction*, Vol. 1, (New York, 1978), 19.

[50] *Ibid.*, 59.

[51] Delumeau, *L'Aveu et le pardon*, 5-6.

> a literature ordered according to the infinite task of extracting from the depths of oneself, in between the words, a truth which the very form of the confession (*aveu*) holds out like a shimmering mirage (*comme l'inaccessible*).[52]

Within the eighteenth century, Rousseau's *Confessions* are perhaps one of the best examples of this kind of literature, and moreover some passages of the book are devoted to the confession of masturbation.

The fact that obligatory confession was suppressed by the Reformation, and that this suppression "certainly contributed to the success of the Reformation,"[53] does not mean that Protestants were outside of our "singularly confessing society."[54] Although confession is a Catholic ritual, its influence went far beyond the scope of religion: "Western man has become a confessing animal."[55] The religious practice of confession made possible a dialogue about a solitary practice, allowing for the creation of a power relationship, first between confessors and believers, and later between physicians and patients. This historical shift of authority from confessor to physician of course had consequences on the concrete practice of confession.

Jean Gerson, in the fifteenth century, wondered how to extract from the heart of the young guilty men "the abominable pus of this revolting sin that we call masturbation."[56] He suggested using a typical cross-examination to help confessors to be "clever and circumspect" in order to get a result.[57] He knew that the confession of carnal sins "can be extracted from most people only with extreme difficulty."[58] In the same vein, Saint François Xavier (1506-1552) wrote that the confessor had to imitate "the dexterity of midwives."[59] The confessional system, with its detailed directions for use, became, thanks to the Catholic Church, a subtle know-how in the hands of the confessor.

Medicine brought the sinful connotations of masturbation on the visible surface of the body making verbal confession less necessary:

---

[52] Foucault, *The History of Sexuality*, Vol. 1, 59.

[53] Delumeau, *Un chemin d'histoire* , 173.

[54] Foucault, *The History of Sexuality*, Vol. 1, 59.

[55] *Ibid.*

[56] Gerson, "De Confessione Mollitiei," in *Œuvre complète, Volume VIII, L'Œuvre spirituelle et pastorale*, 71.

[57] *Ibid.* See also Stengers and van Neck, *Histoire d'une grande peur*, 30.

[58] Quoted in Delumeau, *L'Aveu et le pardon*, 19.

[59] Quoted in *ibid.*, 23.

from then on it was possible to read on the faces and the bodies the signs of the sin. In *L'Onanisme*, Tissot explains how he listened to a patient's description of his troubles: weak legs, pain in the back, etc. These clues were sufficient for Tissot: "I solicited from him strongly to confess to me if he had ever soiled himself with the abominable crime of Onan."[60] Vomitings, a weakening of the organs of respiration, a "total slackening in the nervous system (*genre nerveux*)," and a "prodigious weakening of the organs of generation"[61] were the signs of a sinful habit. With religion, the confessor developed the art of confessing; with medicine, the sins perspired through the patient's body, and it was the organs of the body that went to confess.

But Tissot had no trouble getting his patients to confess verbally, perhaps because the fear of death in the eighteenth century was graver than the fear of Hell.[62] His patients liked to confess through the letters they wrote to him,[63] in which they described in great detail their diseases and their lives, sometimes writing in Latin when they reached the subject of their sexual activities. Tissot even wrote in the preface of some editions of *L'Onanisme* that he did not want to reply anymore to the letters written by people who masturbate because "they are so many of them that if [he] wanted to reply to all of them, they would take all [his] time."[64]

A Shadow in the Enlightenment

Masturbation "became a Protestant version of a "mortal sin," the unofficial Eleventh Commandment, Thou Shalt Not Commit Self-Pollution, at the risk of life and health.'"[65] Since God manifested Himself in nature, to follow this Eleventh Commandment meant conforming to the wisdom of natural law. The eighteenth century was indeed preoccupied with the idea of nature and assumed the existence of a universal human being, while its travel accounts

---

[60] *Ibid.*, 114.

[61] *Ibid.*, 46-47.

[62] See Walker, *The Decline of Hell.*

[63] Consultations by letter were common in the eighteenth century: "The Age of the Enlightenment was also the age of consulting by letter *par excellence*." Brockliss, "Consultation by Letter in Early Eighteenth-Century Paris: The Medical Practice of Etienne-François Geoffroy," in *French Medical Culture in the 19th Century*, 80.

[64] Tissot, *L'Onanisme*, 20.

[65] J. Donat, "Introduction" to *John Wesley's Thoughts on the Sin of Onan.*

discovered such diverse people as Indians, Tahitians, or Eskimos. It may be that "the Enlightenment [needed] to believe in human nature," because the "human being [had] no other aims than the accomplishment of his nature" to reach happiness.[66] "It [was] nature, in the final analysis, that [had] to guarantee happiness,"[67] for it had a double function: "to reveal to man what he has to do and how he can be happy, both being combined by a necessary relation."[68] With its divine connotation, the idea of nature expressed what is and what should be: "an idea both positive and normative."[69] It was peculiar to the eighteenth century to believe in the "art of being happy" and happiness was a "key idea" in the Enlightenment,[70] and the path to follow was science:

> I dare then say without prejudice in favor of letters and sciences, that it is they which make a nation flourish, and which spread throughout the heart of men the rules of the upright reason and the seeds of gentleness, virtue and humanity so necessary for the happiness of society.[71]

This quotation from Diderot and d'Alembert's *Encyclopédie* is an example of how letters and science were idealized by the eighteenth century Enlightenment; they should bring happiness because they liberate humanity from superstitions and aim the spotlight of truth at the nature of human beings. As an historian like Peter Gay says, "if there was any real hope for man, it was science that would realize it."[72]

Was this hope fulfilled? Gay thinks that the answer to this question is "yes." He writes that "generosity was a luxury a progressive society could afford;"[73] that Fénelon's compassion, expressed in his denunciation of war and brutality in 1699, became "commonplace" a few decades later;[74] and ends in saying: "critics have often wondered that men of the eighteenth century should have been optimists; we should rather wonder how they could have been anything else."[75]

---

[66] Ehrard, *L'Idée de nature en France*, 251-252.

[67] Mauzi, *L'Idée du bonheur dans la littérature et la pensée française au XVIIIème siècle*, 559.

[68] *Ibid.*, 563.

[69] Ehrard, *L'Idée de nature en France*, 792. See also Krieger, *Kings and Philosophers, 1689-1789*, 163.

[70] Mauzi, *L'Idée du bonheur*, 13.

[74] Gay, *The Enlightenment: An Interpretation, The Science of Freedom*, 124.

[73] *Ibid.*, 30.

[74] *Ibid.*, 36-37.

[75] *Ibid.*, 38.

However he tempers his enthusiasm with a footnote, where he refers to Voltaire's anti-Semitism as an illustration of the fact that "the age of Enlightenment was far from perfect."[76]

It is not difficult to find other loathsome examples in the same vein of Voltaire's anti-Semitism such as sweatshops or child labor. And one can wonder if a statement such as "the age of criticism was also an age of humanity,"[77] is not so vague as to be void of meaning. Moreover, it appears that the implicit causal link drawn by Gay between reason and humanity remains intact with the example of Voltaire's anti-Semitism, for the latter had nothing to do with reason. *L'Onanisme*, on the other hand, is illustrative of a reason that does have an intrinsic element of shadow.

Tissot wanted his medicine to be a real science, for which he needed knowledge and experience gained through selfless dedication to the work: "The greatest physicians...sacrificed the finest times of their life for a sustained and assiduous study of the human body."[78] In *L'Onanisme*, he tried to set his book apart from its famous English predecessor *Onania*, written some fifty years before. The ideas in *Onania* were, according to Tissot, only "theological and moral trivialities."[79] In comparison to this "real chaos," *L'Onanisme* was a book of science. It had a logical theory, based on a prestigious medical tradition, and many observations that proved by experience the truth of its theory. It is far from what we call a scientific book today, for it lacks statistical or quantitative analysis, but it was considered a scientific book in the eighteenth century: "measured by eighteenth-century physiological and biological standards, Tissot's work was sound science."[80]

But was the aim of *L'Onanisme* to bring happiness? At first sight, it may seem that it is rather the opposite that is true, since Tissot said that in writing about mortal diseases instead of writing about mortal sins, his intention was to frighten more effectively everyone who masturbated: "when one knows men, one persuades oneself easily that it is easier to divert them from their vice through the fear of a

[76] *Ibid.*

[77] *Ibid.*, 29.

[78] Tissot, *Avis au peuple*, 382.

[79] Tissot, *L'Onanisme*, 41.

[80] Mortier, Colen, and Simon, "Inner-scientific Reconstructions in the Discourse on Masturbation (1760-1950)," in *Paedagogica Historica: International Journal of the History of Education*, Tome XXX, 1994 (3), 846.

present harm, than through a reasoning based on principles whose truth one does not take enough care to inculcate."[81] Tissot alluded to Molière's *Le Mariage Forcé* for showing that sometimes a whack is useful for get someone believe in something: "Marphurius doubted of everything, Scanarelle whacked him, and he believed."[82] However, it would be a misreading of *L'Onanisme* to say that Tissot's goal was to create a diffuse feeling of fear. Rather, Tissot wanted to fight against what he thought to be a mortal epidemic and wrote his book because he thought it would be "useful...for humanity."[83] He believed that masturbation "takes perhaps a more terrible toll than smallpox."[84]

Tissot was more a philanthropic physician than a sadistic one. When we consider his entire life and work, it is more likely that his aim was humanistic, even though he wanted to frighten his readers, the end justifying the means. He treated the rich as well as the poor, but the latter—who called him *le Bon Dieu de Lausanne*—he treated for free.[85] Consistent with this philanthropic attitude, Tissot was also "among the first to denounce malnutrition and over-work as a factor, in the masses' poor health, tightly connected in a vicious circle to their poverty."[86]

But the fact remains that Tissot's philanthropy created a terror that was to last for more than a century. Moreover, it seems that this terror was much more frightening than the one created by religion. Dutoit-Membrini, the minister from Lausanne who also wrote a book against masturbation, had, like Tissot, the feeling that masturbation was a bad thing, but he wanted to speak from a religious viewpoint. His book was published the same year, in the same place, and with the same editor as the first edition of *L'Onanisme*, but was soon completely forgotten, the opposite of what happened to Tissot's book. The role of bringing fear to the world was now in the hands of medicine, "the vocation for working on the conservation of humanity."[87] How can we explain this irony? And why did *L'Onanisme* become such an influential best-seller?

---

[81] Tissot, *L'Onanisme*, 17.

[82] *Ibid.*

[83] *Ibid.*, 15.

[84] *Ibid.*, 19.

[85] Teysseire and Verry-Jolivet, "Présentation" to *Avis au peuple*, 11, 14.

[86] Emch-Dériaz, *Tissot*, 4.

[87] Tissot, *Avis au peuple*, 48.

One reason may be because *L'Onanisme* was clearly and rationally written and intelligible to the general educated public. It was exactly what the Enlightenment was asking for—a scientific discourse without "theological and moral trivialities," based on facts, logic, and a prestigious medical tradition. Another reason for its success may be that, although *L'Onanisme* represented a revolution in the form of the arguments, Tissot used other words to argue basically the same thing that the Church had claimed for centuries: masturbation is dangerous. Using the terminology of the Enlightenment, he confirmed a well established prejudice against masturbation that was shared by most of the people of the eighteenth century, whether they were religious or not.

Yet another reason may be that *L'Onanisme* could be used by the enlightened elite to fight against depopulation, supposedly a problem of the time, and it served the "bio-politics of the population."[88] Even if the *philosophes* had not shared Tissot's belief, they were aware of the consequences of masturbation as a threat to the survival of the human species. A distinction has to be made between the contents of *L'Onanisme* and what some of the eighteenth century readers took from it. Tissot did not insist that his book could save humanity. In fact, he was more concerned about individuals. Of course, in saving individuals, in saving them from sterility[89] or from becoming uninterested in the "legitimate pleasures of the nuptial bond," he was contributing to the effort to save humanity from depopulation. He thought that depopulation was "a truth of fact (*vérité de fait*) that strikes everybody."[90] But the fact remains that *L'Onanisme* is about the diseases brought on by masturbation and their rational explanations, not about the danger of depopulation.

Some used *L'Onanisme* as an argument against chastity, not only to counter depopulation but to counter the power of the Church. For example Voltaire commented on *L'Onanisme* that there were as many people ill from retaining their semen as from losing too much of it.[91] Voltaire's "misreading" may have been due to the fact that the fight against depopulation was linked to the fight against the Church; de Lignac, Voltaire, Diderot, Rousseau, or Buffon were all against

[88] Foucault, *The History of Sexuality*, Vol. 1, 139.

[89] Tissot, *L'Onanisme*, 43.

[90] Tissot, *Avis au peuple*, 44.

[91] Voltaire, "Onan, onanisme," *Œuvre complètes de Voltaire, Dictionnaire philosophique*, Tome VII, (Paris, 1826), 196.

religious chastity because it was an obstacle to the reproduction of the species.[92] "Sex was a means of access both to the life of the body and the life of the species,"[93] as Foucault argues. But the content of *L'Onanisme* weighed much more on the side of the life of the body, while enlightened readers like Voltaire emphasized the life of the species, producing in this way an important reason for the enlightened public to buy, read, comment, and quote from the book. And the fact that people were less afraid of Hell than before made a scientific discourse guaranteeing death instead of a Divine punishment more impressive than a religious belief threatening a Divine punishment. All of which contributed to the popularity of the book.

Several letters from patients show that Tissot's discourse was firmly internalized by the culture. The masturbators could not doubt it was their abominable practice that was responsible for their multiple symptoms. For instance, Rossary, a 25-year-old man who consulted Tissot in Paris, wrote that he suffered from an "extreme weakening of memory," from a "difficulty to breath," from an "extreme sensibility to hot and cold," from "hoarseness," his nervous system (*genre nerveux*) was in an "extreme slackening," his stomach was "weak," his face was pale.[94] All these symptoms can be found in *L'Onanisme* and often in almost the same terms. It is interesting to note that Rossary and other patients were not openly referring to *L'Onanisme* while listing their symptoms. Many were unaware of the influence that the book had on them, unaware of the fact that it made them focus on some specific parts or functions of the body and not on others.

The new scientific discourse was more difficult to ignore than the previous religious one, because it brought a new coercive power onto the scene—not an external power but an internal one. It was not God who was threatening the patients but their own reason. The great strength of scientific discourses, which is missing in religious discourses, lies in the fact that they are able to make believe that no subject speaks except the objective truth. From the patient's viewpoint, it is not Tissot who decides to punish or to console; it is not even God or nature; it is, in fact, no external person, for it is not a question of decision but of deduction. If someone who masturbates

---

[92] Tarczylo, *Sexe et liberté*, 173-174.

[93] Foucault, *The History of Sexuality*, Vol. 1, 146.

[94] Letter IS 3784/II/144.02.04.11, dated June 13th, 1774.

becomes ill, it is not because the physician, God, or nature have decided to punish him. It is because this is the logical consequence of masturbation. In other words, *L'Onanisme* had such a strong impact on readers because the power relationship was not between Tissot and his patients, but rather between the latter and what they thought was the truth.

There is a coercive power intrinsic in any scientific discourse, a power that has been responsible, in Tissot's case, for more than one and a half century of terror, instead of the happiness promised by science and reason. Instead of having been a soteriology, as expected, science gave an ancient fear a façade of truth which, until then, was missing. In this way a science that was supposed to enlighten became a blinding light that would not be dimmed until much later.

Bibliography

Alembert, Jean Le Rond d'. "Discours préliminaire des éditeurs." *Encyclopédie, ou Dictionnaire Raisonné des Sciences, des Arts et des Métiers.* Vol. 1. Paris: Chez Briasson; David l'Aîné; Le Breton; Durand, 1751, i-Lij.

Anonymous. *Onania, or the Heinous Sin of Self-Pollution, and All its Frightful Consequences, in Both Sexes, Consider'd, with Spiritual and Physical Advice to Those, Who Have Already Injur'd Themselves by this Abominable Practice.* (First published in London, 1715?) New York: Garland Publishing, Inc., 1986.

Anonymous. "Lettres." *Encyclopédie, ou Dictionnaire Raisonné des Sciences, des Arts et des Métiers.* Vol. 9. Paris: Chez Briasson; David l'Aîné; Le Breton; Durand, 1765.

Brockliss, Laurence. "Consultation by Letter in Early Eighteenth-Century Paris: The Medical Practice of Etienne-François Geoffroy." *French Medical Culture in the 19th Century.* Eds. Ann La Berge and Mordechai Feingold. Amsterdam: Rodopi, 1994.

Bullough, Vern L. *Sexual Variance in Society and History.* Chicago: The University of Chicago Press, 1976.

Chambaud, Ménuret de. "Manstupration." *Encyclopédie, ou Dictionnaire Raisonné des Sciences, des Arts et des Métiers.* Vol. 10. Paris: Chez Briasson; David l'Aîné; Le Breton; Durand, 1765.

Delumeau, Jean. *Un Chemin d'Histoire.* Paris: Fayard, 1981.

____________. *L'Aveu et le Pardon.* Paris: Fayard, 1990.

Diderot, Denis. "Explication du Frontispice de L'Encyclopédie." *Encyclopédie, ou Dictionnaire Raisonné des Sciences, des Arts et des Métiers.* Vol. 1. Paris: Chez Briasson; David l'Aîné; Le Breton; Durand, 1751.

Donat, James. "Introduction." *John Wesley's Thoughts on the Sin of Onan: a Critical Edition.* Forthcoming.

Dutoit-Membrini, Jean Philippe. *De l'Onanisme, ou Discours Philosophique et Moral sur la Luxure Artificielle et sur tous les Crimes Relatifs.* Lausanne: De L'Imprimerie d'Antoine Chapuis, 1760.

Ehrard, Jean. *L'Idée de Nature en France dans la Première Moitié du XVIIIème Siècle.* Chambéry: Imprimeries Réunies, 1963.

Emch-Dériaz, Antoinette. *Tissot Physician of the Enlightenment.* New York: Peter Lang, 1992.

Foucault, Michel. *Discipline and Punish.* Trans. Alan Sheridan. New York: Vintage, 1977.

____________. *The History of Sexuality.* Vol. 1. Trans. Robert Hurley. New York: Vintage, 1978.

Galen. "*De Locis Affectis.*" *Claudii Galeni Opera Omnia.* Bk. 6. K VIII. Ed. C. G. Kuehn. Leipzig: Cnoblauch, 1824.

Gay, Peter. *The Enlightenment: An Interpretation.* New York: Norton, 1969.

Gerson, Jean. "De Confessione Mollitiei." *Œuvre Complète. L'Œuvre Spirituelle et Pastorale.* Vol. VIII. Paris: Desclée & Cie, 1971.

Goldstein, Jan. "Foucault and the Post-Revolutionary Self: The Uses of Cousinian Pedagogy in Nineteenth-Century France." *Foucault and the Writing of History.* Ed. Jan Goldstein. Cambridge: Blackwell, 1995.

Hurteau, Pierre. "Catholic Moral Discourse on Male Sodomy and Masturbation in the Seventeenth and Eighteenth Centuries." *Journal of the History of Sexuality.* Chicago: The University of Chicago Press, vol.4, number 1 (July 1993): 1-26.

Jordanova, Ludmilla. "The Popularization of Medecine: Tissot on Onanism." *Textual Practice.* Vol.1, number 1 (Spring 1987).

Kant, Immanuel. *Kant on Education.* Trans. Annette Churton. Bristol: Thoemmes Press, 1992.

Krieger, Leonard. *Kings and Philosophers, 1689-1789.* New York: Norton, 1970.

Larousse, Pierre. "Masturbation." *Grand Dictionnaire Universel du XIXème Siècle* Tome X. Paris: 1873.

Lignac, Louis François Luc de. *A Physical View of Man and Woman in a State of Marriage.* Trans. from the last edition of M. de Lignac. London (?), 1798.

Mainil, Jean. *Dans les Règles du Plaisir.* Paris: Kimé, 1996.

Mauzi, Robert. *L'Idée du Bonheur dans la Littérature et la Pensée Française au XVIIIème Siècle.* Paris: Armand Colin, 1960.

Mortier, Freddy, Willem Colen and Frank Simon. "Inner-scientific Reconstructions in the Discourse on Masturbation (1760-1950)." In *Paedagogica Historica, International Journal of the History of Education.* Tome XXX, 1994 (3).

Rosario, Vernon A. "Phantastical Pollutions: The Public Threat of Private Vice in France." *Solitary Pleasures.* Eds. Paula Bennett and Vernon A. Rosario. New York: Routledge, 1995.

Rousseau, Jean-Jacques. *Les Confessions. Œuvres Complètes,* I. Paris: Gallimard, coll. Bibliothèque de la Pléiade, 1959.

____________. *Discours sur l'Origine et les Fondemens de l'Inégalité Parmi les Hommes. Œuvres Complètes,* III. Paris: Gallimard, coll. Bibliothèque de la Pléiade, 1964.

____________. *Emile. Œuvres Complètes,* IV. Paris: Gallimard, coll. Bibliothèque de la Pléiade, 1969.

____________. *Correspondance Complète de Jean Jacques Rousseau.* Tome XI, Juin-Juillet 1762. Genève: Institut et Musée Voltaire, 1970.

____________. *Correspondance Complète de Jean-Jacques Rousseau.* Tome XII, Juillet-Août 1762. Genève: Institut et Musée Voltaire, 1970.

__________________. "Correspondance de Jean-Jacques Rousseau et du Médecin Tissot." *Annales de la Société Jean-Jacques Rousseau.* Tome septième. Genève: A. Jullien, 1911, 19-40.

Starobinski, Jean. *L'Œil vivant.* Paris: Gallimard, 1961.

Stengers, Jean, and Anne van Neck. *Histoire d'une Grande Peur, la Masturbation.* Institut Synthélabo pour le Progrès de la Connaissance, coll. Les Empêcheurs de Penser en Rond, 1998.

Tarczylo, Théodore. *Sexe et Liberté au Siècle des Lumières.* Paris: Presses de la Renaissance, 1983.

__________________. "Prêtons la Main à la Nature: l'Onanisme de Tissot." *Dix-Huitième Siècle,* 12 (1980), 79-96.

Teysseire, Daniel, and Verry-Jolivet, Corinne. Présentation to *Avis au peuple sur sa Santé,* by Samuel-Auguste-André-David Tissot. Paris: Quai Voltaire, Edima, Cité des Sciences et de l'Industrie, 1993.

Tissot, Samuel-Auguste-André-David. *L'Onanisme.* Paris: Editions de la Différence, 1991.

__________________. *Avis au Peuple sur sa Santé.* Paris: Quai Voltaire, Edima, Cité des Sciences et de l'Industrie, 1993.

__________________. *De la Santé des Gens de Lettres.* Paris: Editions de la Différence, 1991.

Voltaire, François-Marie Arouet de. "Onan, Onanisme." *Œuvre Complètes de Voltaire, Dictionnaire Philosophique.* Tome VII. Paris: Baudouin Frères, 1826.

Walker, D. P. *The Decline of Hell.* London: Routledge & Kegan Paul, 1964.

Wesley, John. *John Wesley's Thoughts on the Sin of Onan: A Critical Edition.* Forthcoming.

THE A.D.D. PROJECT

RON SCHNEEBAUM

After almost twenty years in medicine, I see that, while modern medicine has worked out intricate models and treatment plans for the illnesses that face us, the human heart has been left out of the picture. The intuitive knowledge that a loving wisdom permeates our lives has been completely ignored. Without love, in its deepest and highest meaning, I do not believe that we can successfully solve the riddles that face us. I will use the analogy of walking to underline our need for balance. When we walk we put our weight on one foot and then the other. If we did not alternate the foot that bears weight, if we favored one foot over the other, we would move along awkwardly. Eventually we would break down. This describes what is happening to our society. We have exclusively relied on the foot of scientific thinking. The scientific approach created modern culture's institutions, its direction, and its dreams. For the sake of our analogy, we will call the approach to knowledge that employs the scientific method the foot of "knowing." If we wish to

Ron Schneebaum is a pediatrician, a fellow of the American Academy of Pediatrics, and a former elementary school teacher who lives in Carlisle, Massachusetts. In addition to his medical degree, he holds a master's degree in education. He founded the A.D.D. Project in 1998 and Center Reach Counseling in 1999.

go forward humanely, with rhythm and grace, we need to elevate that foot and walk on the opposite one. We will call that opposite foot, "not knowing." Using our analogy to look at the diagnosis and treatment of Attention Deficit Disorder, we will see that our current understanding is based on one foot: the foot of science. Our approach to this disorder needs balance. Our children ask for and deserve our attention to this matter.

Sixty years ago Ritalin was mostly used to treat narcolepsy, a condition characterized by brief involuntary attacks of sleep. A physician noted that Ritalin—or amphetamines (a family of drugs with chemical similarities to Ritalin)—had a calming effect in some patients who were active and difficult to manage children. These active children were thought (as it was then termed) to have a "Minimal Brain Dysfunction." Medication seemed a better choice for this group of children than the juvenile delinquency that awaited them. Ritalin/amphetamines were then given to children who were impulsive and hyperactive in school but whose behavior was not extreme. These medications had the same effect—increased attention and decreased distractibility. The term Minimal Brain Dysfunction did not seem to fit for these children, and a new name, Attention Deficit Disorder, was coined. The name was later changed to its current ADHD (Attention Deficit Hyperactivity Disorder) to reflect the hyperactivity that can be seen as well as the attention deficits. The diagnosis of ADHD was (and remains) descriptive in nature. The diagnosis is made when a child has a history of decreased attention, hyperactivity, impulsivity, or any combination of the three, not attributable to medical, psychiatric, or psychosocial problems.

A dramatic increase in the use of medication for these children occurred in the early 1990s after a subgroup of children—those who had ADHD without hyperactivity—began to be regularly treated with medication. The subgroup was not performing up to expectations in school, and they were considered daydreamers. It was reasoned that they had ADHD without hyperactivity because they were "inwardly" rather than "outwardly" hyperactive. The use of Ritalin/amphetamines enhanced their school performance, and the floodgates were thrown open. The number of prescriptions of Ritalin/amphetamines for children in this country continues to skyrocket.

The increase in diagnosis of ADD has not been limited to children. The prevailing wisdom once was that the condition resolved on its own by the end of the teenage years. This view also changed in the 1990s. In 1995 Dr. Ned Hallowell wrote his first book, *Driven to Distraction*, and described in detail how ADD appears in adults. The book hit the best-seller lists across the country. Adults who functioned at a level less than expected and had the same features as children with ADHD began to be diagnosed and treated with Ritalin/amphetamines.

Science searched for a model, an explanation, for ADD. It was reasoned that the brain has a central processing center that is dedicated to attention. Because of this well-working system, extraneous material can be ignored and attention may be focused. A pilot in a storm, for example, can land an airplane and ignore any distracting input. Neurotransmitters—chemical substances in the brain—were to bring messages from one area of the brain to another. It was explained that the children and adults with ADD have a decrease in specific neurotransmitters. They have enough to focus on what appeals to them, they just do not have enough for routine activity. The medication, though it is not clear how, replaces the missing neurotransmitters. From this standpoint there is nothing wrong with medication. It simply makes these people equal to the others who do not have the deficit. Doctors, then, would liken giving the medication to giving someone eyeglasses. It doesn't change who they are; it simply gives them back what should be their innate ability. Now here is a tidy package: a diagnosis with criteria for who fits and who does not, a treatment plan, and a scientific model that explains the cause and mechanism of treatment.

More scientific work is currently under way. Some researchers are trying to understand the genetics of the disease. Others are trying to find the place(s) in the brain of the specific defect(s). Huge efforts are being put into developing drugs that would increase neurotransmitter levels with fewer side effects. The financial reward for the makers of such a drug would be astounding, as some two million prescriptions for Ritalin have been written, and the number continues to increase dramatically. The scientific model generated it all: an observation, experimentation with medication, a hypothesis explaining the observed phenomenon, and a path for further research. The only matter is to find and treat those with the disorder so that everyone will be on an equal level and perform maximally. Support groups abound. A battle is now being waged to recognize the disorder under the Americans with Disabilities Act so that the afflicted will get needed services. It is fully legitimized.

However, complex questions arise the more one examines this diagnosis and its treatment. Some facts about ADD and its treatment are startling. Current estimates are that ten percent of the population (or one out of every six boys), is affected with ADD. This number is routinely accepted in the professional literature. If ten percent of the population in this country needs drugs to function optimally, are we describing a disorder or making a statement about our society? It is known that Ritalin and amphetamines will help anyone concentrate, ADHD or not. This complicates the mater. For if everyone could have increased concentration by taking these medications, who should decide which students and athletes get prescriptions and which do not? Further, if these drugs really are so benign, why wouldn't we want to make them more widely available? Is it because we instinctively feel that something about it is wrong?

Thirty years ago amphetamines were a menace. The word was "speed kills." Many people became addicted. Now we are saying that it or its cousin should be prescribed routinely for children as young as kindergartners, and the long term effects of this approach on such a wide scale are unknown. While we implore students to, "Say no to drugs," we are prescribing Ritalin/amphetamines for children with ADHD so that certain social situations will be easier for them. The message about drug use becomes confusing. When these children have to decide whether or not to "say no," will they have learned which drugs that make social situations easier are okay?

Imagine being told, as many children are, "We're going to see grandma today. Take your Ritalin before we go. You know how upset she gets when you don't behave." We are telling children from the youngest of ages that they must take medication to function normally without really examining the long term effects of this radical approach to child psychology.

As a medical doctor I have transformed my approach to ADD in the past few years. I was once quite traditional in the way I diagnosed and treated these children: the evaluations in my office were thorough, and if I had questions, I reviewed them with recognized experts in the field. My reputation spread. People came to get my thoughts and opinions, even if their children were not in my practice. But the more I got to know the children I evaluated because of parent or teacher concern and those children who were diagnosed with ADHD, the more I saw that these were great kids. I asked parents to describe the strongest qualities of these children. Kind, sensitive, insightful, enthusiastic, lover of nature, were the words used to describe them in more than ninety-five percent of the cases I reviewed. I began to call it, "Enthusiasm and Love of Life Disorder" and began to think these children were not the ones with the problem.

These children had some of the traits we work so hard to cultivate in young people, and yet we were putting them on medication to change them. I began to wonder why. The common assertion that they had a neurological disorder for which medication was the answer no longer fit, and I began to look for new answers. Some of the children in my practice were diagnosed with ADHD by other authorities and would have been so diagnosed at the office of anyone who treats children for ADHD. Their stories are typical.

One seventeen year old had the best summer of his life in a wilderness survival program.[1] He came back exhilarated. He learned about who he was and what he valued by confronting physical challenges in a natural setting. When he came back he saw his friends and his activities from this heightened perspective. However, this window of opportunity closed rapidly. School started, and he fell back into his former routines. School was not motivating. He was eventually referred to a psychiatrist who put him on both Ritalin and an antidepressant.

A great many children and young adults with ADHD find wonder and renewal in nature. Often school teachers and officials do not recognize this. Learning takes place indoors for six hours a day and assignments at home often take another few hours. This goes on for ten months a year and some people want this extended. Even some of the world's greatest thinkers found this schedule difficult and limiting. For example Gandhi said of his school days that, "they were the most miserable years of my life." He had no aptitude for lessons and rarely appreciated his teachers.[2]

An eighth grader came to me because of concerns raised by his school teachers. He was not performing up to expectations. When we spoke in private, I was impressed with his thoughtfulness, his sincerity, and his intelligence. Little of what he saw in his teachers,

[1] Some details have been changed to protect patient privacy.

[2] This and descriptions of famous people and their connection to school are from James Hillman, *The Soul's Code* (New York: HarperCollins, 1999).

texts, or school assignments touched the issues important in his life. Even though he was told that he needed to learn the assigned material for later success, it was not enough for him. He could have done the work but just did not see the point. I knew that medication would help him be more attentive (and medication would have been prescribed by most other physicians), but I was not sure that I would be doing him a favor. I thought of Einstein, who was a terrible student and wrote of his school experiences: "I preferred to endure all sorts of punishments rather than to learn gabble by rote."

One girl I have known since her birth is typical of others who are diagnosed with ADHD. She was a demanding first child who unsettled her indulgent parents. As she grew older her parents became frustrated. At times they would yell before they gave in. But she was sweet and fun loving and had a remarkable sparkle in her eyes. I wanted the parents to seek help because they held differing views about child rearing—frequently one was away overnight because of work. I knew that sooner or later the issue of ADHD would be raised because of her inability to do anything that went against her grain. Eventually a surgeon they knew recommended they take the girl to see a neurologist at one of Boston's prestigious hospitals. The father was not at the appointment, and I was not called or consulted. After a forty-five minute visit, a prescription for Ritalin was written. Medication and its dosing became the focus of this child's behavior management, and a chance to understand her needs and her family's dynamics was missed.

Some strong-willed children end up with the diagnosis of ADHD. One little girl in my practice is a born leader, and her mother sensed this immediately after her birth. Raising the girl has been a real challenge, though with firm, loving, and gentle patience, she has made progress. Now the girl is in second grade, and the school is suggesting that she be evaluated for ADHD because she has difficulty sitting quietly during "circle time." Her mother, who feels that the girl needs greater mental and physical challenges, asked whether her child might spend time working with the school's maintenance team. This suggestion was accepted by the school, and it has worked wonders for her. This is perhaps a blessing: Eleanor Roosevelt was so headstrong when she was young that she was impossible to live with.

Children who have been diagnosed with ADHD often excel in other activities. While they have difficulty sticking with things that do not interest them, they often have great tenacity for that which they love. Many accomplished musicians and artists who are diagnosed with ADHD practice for hours on end, but schoolwork does not captivate them the same way. This, too, has historically been seen with great artists. Picasso left school at the age of ten. He could not remember the sequence of the alphabet or learn arithmetic as a boy. He only wanted to paint.

We cannot understand the majority of children who have the diagnosis of ADHD or ADD completely without examining our schools. The driving force behind our present system of education is simple and straight forward: certain skills must be learned if today's students are to find a place in the job market of tomorrow. Our nation's best and brightest must excel in science and math if we are to maintain our dominance in technology and business. Every student in the country is expected to learn certain material by the end of each school year. There is little room for difference or failure. Students are considered akin to machines, taking in certain information so they can move along in the system.

A teacher's love for a subject can no longer be his or her guiding star. Required curriculum has become the master, replacing enthusiasm when necessary. A teacher may follow the interests of a class to a certain degree, but the material covered cannot go too far astray. Teaching in an unorthodox fashion faces these same strict limits. Our current method of educating children began near the turn of the twentieth century when our nation was still expanding its borders, and we were struggling to assimilate millions of immigrants. Rigidity and uniformity in education might have had a place then, but its dominant role is outdated.

Let's look at our present approach to education from another angle and give it a simple test. Since the majority of people in our country have been educated in this school system, and since the basic direction of this system has not significantly changed in the past hundred years, the society its graduates have produced is as an objective measure of the success of its approach. With such a test we should see exactly what we expected. The scientific and technological achievements are astounding. We have literally changed the face of the earth. However, these achievements have led to problems greater than we have ever faced. Our earth, the atmosphere, the air we breathe, and the water we drink are in grave danger. We complain that we do not have time for the things that matter most. We are less happy with the course of our daily lives and feel we have less control over it. We are becoming less compassionate. Those who do not have access to money and power are becoming further removed from those who do.

Why is this relevant to the diagnosis and treatment of ADHD? It is because we put so much faith and believe so strongly in the correctness of this system of education that we are willing to medicate our children and let doctors tell us that they have brain defects, because they are not working hard enough in school. If we truly want our children to be kind, loving, and creative, we must ask why we are giving them drugs that enhance a certain kind of practicality, when it is possible that these drugs perform at the expense of the very traits we cherish.

We need answers that are inspired and come from a different source.[3] The time has come to listen to our hearts and act on what we know is right. The time has come to take a stand. Our children expect it. Our world depends on it.

---

[3] *Editors' Note*: Ron Schneebaum and his collaborator, Julie Pierce, have more information available for parents, educators, physicians, teenagers, and children diagnosed with ADHD. They can be contacted at: The A.D.D. Project, P.O. Box 542, Carlisle, MA, 01741 or at www.addproject.org.

Teenage Goths: The Bearable Darkness of Being

COLETTE KAVANAGH

> Grounds for an unusually intense fear of death are nowadays not far to seek; they are obvious enough, the more so as all life that is senselessly wasted and misdirected means death, too. This may account for the unnatural intensification of the fear of death in our time, when life has lost its deeper meaning for so many people, forcing them to exchange the life-preserving rhythm of the aeons for the dread(ed) ticking of the clock.
>
> —C. G. Jung, *Civilization In Transition* (368)

The world as we know it is ending. Endings can intensify anxiety and fear. One hears talk of the end of art, culture, nature, and even the end of our human existence, as we constellate death in many forms. Throughout the Western world and as far away as Australia and South Africa, a teenage subculture—the Goth movement—has thrived on the fantasy of death. Many teenagers, feeling confused and misunderstood, suffer from anxiety and depression. Through rebellion, experimentation, and "acting out" different

Colette Kavanagh was raised in Ireland and attended the Swedish College of Arts & Design in Stockholm. After travelling extensively making documentary films, and a career in business in Amsterdam, she now is completing a doctorate in mythological studies at Pacifica Graduate Institute in Santa Barbara, California.

life-styles, they learn to become independent adults, differentiating themselves from their parents. To the outer world Goths look like "lost souls," but the Goth movement enables young people to give form and expression to these difficult emotions, making them visible in creative, nondestructive ways. There they find community—a sense of kinship and fun with other Goths—which enables them to transform depression into melancholy and the "dark" into "a darker light."

James Hillman, in a seminar entitled, "In Defense of Melancholia," referred to the often neglected gods of melancholy:

> Melancholy is a given with the planet, and it needs to be cared for. If not, it becomes clinical depression. As Jung says, the gods have become diseases, and the neglected gods of Melancholy become Depression. The job is to revert depression back to melancholy, not to cure depression, not to lift depression and make us "happy," but to increase our understanding of melancholia; the area of mood, beauty, longing, nostalgia, sadness, and despair.

Goths are melancholic but generally not depressed. Melancholy is a creative state rich in images. Depression involves loss of Eros, imagination, and creativity. It often involves not caring about one's physical appearance or any other aspect of the daily round. In contrast melancholy looks into the shadows and sees not only what society would ignore but recognizes the beauty and wonder in what is rejected. Goths tend to like the night. This is because the night makes everything look different, and people and things can seemingly become more beautiful or mysterious in the dark. Moonlight changes the way things look, and in the dark you use your imagination more, filling in the blank spaces created by shadows.

The ancient Goths came from the island of Gothland (now Gotland) off the coast of Sweden. Their god was the dark and mysterious Odin, god of Twilight, Midnight, and Dawn, who mated with Mother Night. In the *Eddas*, Odin commands a prophetess to rise from her grave as he craves the wisdom she holds of an earlier age now buried and dead. In order to receive this wisdom, he sacrifices himself on the World Tree for nine nights. Through hierogamy (sacred marriage) with this prophetess, Odin is reborn with the gifts of wisdom and poetry. Mircea Eliade claims Odin was the god of necromancy (382).

The Norse Queen of the Underworld, Mother Hel, was also revered by the Goths. She gave her name to the Celtic Lord of Death, *Helman*, who was her companion, and the *Hel-kappe* or *Hel*-met which Northern shamans used to render themselves invisible, like ghosts, enabling them to visit the Underworld and return to earth again without dying. Celtic traditions also give various accounts of an Aes Sidh, or "paradise of the dead," an open world connected by a bridge to the land of the living, sometimes also appearing as an island in the ocean.

Archeological remains indicate that the island of Gothland has been inhabited since neolithic times, and ancient Roman, Arabic, and Anglo Saxon coins have been found there. In approximately 150 C.E. the Goths migrated from Scandinavia and spread throughout Europe, splitting into two groups, the Visigoths and the Ostrogoths. They held high positions in society and formed secret orders.

Subcultures by nature rebel against the status quo, and the modern day Goth movement, derived from the punk movement in the 1970s, is no exception. However, there is one major difference. The punk movement was anarchistic and nihilistic and tried to shock mainstream society through confrontation. Goths do not look for acceptance. Instead, their desire is to be isolated and not be accepted. Their goal is to scare people and be separate, not only from the mainstream culture with its religion, values, beliefs, and way of life, but even from the punk movement with which they might seem to have an affinity.

Goths embrace Western society's shadow—the fear of death and decay. They are fascinated with gothic romance, the mysterious, and the macabre. Their costumes are theatrical and portray a sense of mourning. They wear mostly black, often contrasted with made-up white faces. Their lips are usually colored blood-red or black and some dye their hair red, black, green, or purple. Many wear clothes in the style of past centuries. Men often wear black silk or ruffled shirts, brocade vests, velvet knickers, and lots of jewelry. Bondage clothing—leather collars, corsets, fishnet, lace petticoats, and veils—are also worn, as well as tattered stockings which they wear to signify the beauty of decay.

Sorrel Smith is an artist and illustrator—and a Goth. Her art and writings are both romantic and macabre. An element of tragedy is often present in her drawings, juxtaposed with beauty and decadence.

The characters seem to exist in a realm that is apart from time. Each picture is like a fragment of some strange dream. A conversation with her revealed a voice from behind the Goth "mask of death."

Colette: You are twenty-two now and have been in the Goth movement for several years. It obviously has something special for you. Have you ever thought what it is that you find so special?

Sorrel: Well, I seem to think that it has a romanticism and an appreciation of art that doesn't exist elsewhere in our culture. Our culture is really destitute when it comes to that...and a certain emotional integrity in acceptance of things that are rejected in our culture such as...well, nineteenth century concepts like melancholy and the acceptance of death as part of the natural cycle of life. I think we live in denial. There is a cult of eternal youth going on in our culture, and it's really sick. Goth kids want to get old like anybody else, but there's a consciousness of what I call "keeping your death perception."

Colette: How old were you when you first became a Goth?

Sorrel: Fourteen.

Colette: And how did that happen? Did you meet some Goths?

Sorrel: No, actually it kind of happened spontaneously. A friend of mine and I started wearing black. I had made a Halloween costume that was like a witch's outfit with lots of tatters and black lace hanging out of it...very theatrical looking. I was feeling very angst-ridden at the time. I was really popular in school. This was my first year in high school, and I was really playing the game. I was the blonde "rocker-chick," and everybody liked me, but inside I felt really fake. I had been very lonely my whole childhood. I never found anyone I could relate to, and I still had not found anyone I could relate to.

Colette: Was that because you were an only child or was your soul asking for something else?

Sorrel: No, it didn't matter how many children I met. It was just I couldn't relate to anybody. I was interested in mythology and poetry, and as a fourteen-year-old in America...anywhere...where are you going to meet young people with whom you can share those things? I was already reading Yeats and Tennyson,...and they were just nonexistent.

Colette: Do you think that was partly because your parents were special in giving you that wonderful gift, but part of that gift was separating you from mainstream society and the loneliness that went with it?

Sorrel: Yes. I felt I had no connection with the rest of my culture and certainly not with my own age group.

Colette: And does that loneliness still persist to some extent?

Sorrel: Yes. I've found more people now as I get older, but it's still very slow. But anyway, when I was fourteen, I was still playing the game to be accepted in certain ways. I knew I was different inside, but I didn't want it to show. I hid it as much as possible, until there was a certain breaking point. I don't know what caused it in particular, but I felt I was being completely fake. I was really sad inside and I thought to myself, "What if I show on the outside what I am feeling inside." So I began to wear my Halloween costume to school. I would paint on my face and paint on my body and just do outrageous things. I decided to become a walking piece of performance art, and the natural reaction was nobody wanted to speak to me anymore. But I was so much happier. I felt free.

Colette: How did your teachers react, did they try to change you?

Sorrel: For the most part they could not relate to me at all. I had one art teacher who was very good, who gave me a lot of freedom. I showed her my portfolio, and she told me I did not have to do any of the assignments. I could just use the art supplies and do what I wanted. So that was my outlet. Sometimes everybody else would [limit] freedom and a self-expression. Then one day I met a girl who looked just like me...with lines drawn all over her face. I had purple hair and she had green hair, and we went, "Okay!" So she took me to a Goth club. At that point I was fifteen. I didn't realize that there was a movement, a subculture.

Colette: And where was that Goth club? Was it in San Francisco?

Sorrel: It was called, "The Twilight Zone," in Alameda. When I walked in I was absolutely overwhelmed. I thought, "My God, all these people are like me, they all look like freaks and aliens!" (*laughter*). I just felt totally at home. But I was also very idealistic about it. I thought I'd found a literary movement, and I thought Wow!...since they look like this they must be literary and intelligent. I thought that for years, but then I found out that was not true for many of them, and I became disillusioned. They were into the style. It was a life-style, but there was not much thinking that went on behind it. Eventually, I did meet some friends who did have a deeper understanding and philosophy concerning it, so that really kept me going.

Colette: What is that philosophy?

Sorrel: I think the most essential idea behind the Goth movement is bringing to the surface the sadness that is underneath our whole society and expressing that openly. Most of the Goths I know are well adjusted because they feel more in touch with sadness and mourning and that these are okay feelings, not things that need to be rejected but can be processed in an artistic manner.

Colette: When you say there is a lot of artistic expression, how does that manifest itself in the Gothic movement? Do you come together to share poetry?

Sorrel: I wish that there was more of that. That's what I'm trying to create. There is a club in San Francisco where there are Gothic art shows. Its name is "Roderick's Chamber," called after Roderick from "The Fall of the House of Usher." They have art shows there, a different art show every week.

Colette: Done by Goths?

Sorrel: Yes, done by Goths, for Goths...photography, sculpture, or something like that, so there is always something being presented. You find a whole bunch more artists in the Gothic movement than elsewhere. I think they tend to be very creative people. They at least have the urge and the willingness to bring something out, and even if they don't write or paint or something like that, they express themselves in their outward appearance.

Colette: You are obviously holding a very pure ideal, but how do you personally feel about the Goths who express the more Satanic side?

Sorrel: I don't care for it very much.

Colette: So there is a sort of polarity within the movement?

Sorrel: Yes, there is. A lot of people coming in from the outside run up against the whole "skull-and-crossbones" side of it...very morbid, very reactionary. It started as a post-Punk movement, and you can still see that. Punk has its own philosophy. It's about anarchism and rejection of society and is much more politically oriented. The Goth movement is not political at all. It would be nice if it was more involved in social change, but it's not. It's more about pulling away from society and creating a subculture that has nothing to do with the rest of society...creating a separate little morbid (*laughter*) culture of our own. However, a lot of kids get caught up in, "Oh, I'm spooky," and "now my parents are scared of me," kind of thing.

Colette: It gives them a kind of power, a way to worry their parents.

Sorrel: Yes, exactly, and I went through that, too. It's kind of a natural thing, when you're fourteen or fifteen, and you want to break out of your shell and become something new and different. I think it is a necessary phase to go through.

Colette: Do you meet besides clubs? Do you go to special places?

Sorrel: I was kind of envious in Paris this summer, because they have a Goth pub every week. They go to a certain bar, and it's the Goth night for that bar. They all sit around and drink and talk. We don't have that here, and everyone bemoans that fact. There are cafes where people are likely to show up, but it's never certain...so there really isn't a place. I'm desperate for that kind of thing, desperate. My friends bemoan that they have nowhere to go. My mother said to me if you don't find culture, you have to create it. I really would like to see the Goth movement taking on a more literary aspect. A lot of people in the movement have those interests but don't get together and share it.

Androgyny and transvestitism are prominent in Goth-land. Theatrical transvestism can be imagined as having its roots in shamanic rituals which are then fantasized as the magical and religious origins of theater. Cross-dressing for the shamans was a transcendent expression of human potentiality, suggesting we are more than one gender and it was not to be taken literally, but as symbol. Likewise, it is acceptable for male Goths to wear ribbons, jewelry, dresses, or skirts, and the females find this androgynous look attractive. Sex roles are less clearly defined than in mainstream culture. Many women adopt clothing styles, such as Victorian suits and jackets, that are uniquely masculine yet sensual, portraying a dark sophistication. However, this look is not confined to Goths. Haute couture and mainstream fashion runways as well as "photo spreads" in fashion magazines are often inspired by Goth culture and reflect the deadened senses of modern culture. There is also a resurgence of interest in the Vampire archetype. The archetype's undead presence can be seen not only in the fashion world but in music, literature, television, and movies. Body painting, tattooing, and body piercing are also in vogue, revealing the younger generation's call for ritual and initiation.

Robert Johnson, in his book *Ecstasy*, explains how the collective unconscious manifests itself in unchanging archetypal patterns even in the face of religious or societal opposition:

> The basic forms and patterns of human behavior do not change, they merely put on the clothes and mores of a particular time and place... We can try to repress these archetypes, to drive them underground; but sooner or later they will reemerge. They may come back in an unfamiliar form, but they will be driven by the same archetypal energy. (1x)

Sorrow and melancholy are the language of creativity. Since the days of antiquity many writers, thinkers and artists considered themselves melancholics. Melancholy is where the imaginative powers and creative passions can become manifest. One could say that the melancholic disposition has been found among the literati since Greco-Roman times. The Decadents and Romantics of a century ago understood how beauty can be captivating when mixed with sorrow. The Romantics were in love with suffering and the climax of suffering, was the proximity to death. Modern-day Goths, consciously and unconsciously, carry on these ideas, transforming them into a new romance with death.

The Goth movement is now a worldwide phenomenon with clubs on all six continents. The Goth club is a social sanctuary within which individuals occupy "private" space. Unlike most modern dance clubs, which are overcrowded and involve much body-contact, Goth clubs are designed to protect privacy and isolation from those around them, while still allowing a certain amount of social interaction. Their rules of etiquette dictate accepted ways to interact across spatial confines. Low lighting, flickering candles, and smoke from smoke machines or cigarettes limit visibility, while the scent of exotic cigarettes and incense permeates the air. The music ranges from a harsh, Heavy Metal sound, to a deep, somber form of House Music. Sorrel's description of the Goths' clubs shows how diverse the movement can be.

Sorrel: If you talk to two Goths they might give you a totally different story as to what is going on in the clubs, but the interesting thing is that it really is a subculture in the same way as Rave and Ska and other musical phenomena.

Colette: So music is an important part of the Goth movement?

Sorrel: I'd say music is the important thing dividing different subcultures in America. It's really the big thing whether you are a Rude Boy, a Punk Rocker, a Rockabilly, or a Goth. All these various dominations [sic] are organized by music, what kind of music one listens to. But Goths listen to a wide variety of music.

Colette: Are the lyrics of the music expressing the philosophy of Goths?

Sorrel: In most parts they tend to be very dark. Dark images like "Ophelia." God only knows how many Goth songs there are about Ophelia!—you know, young tragedy. It really runs the gamut. You will find Gothic music that sounds Classical or operatic or Celtic...and then, across the board, there is angry and aggressive Industrial Rock. It runs the gamut.

Colette: I read something about the club Helter Skelter, in Los Angeles, and their desire to be totally sacrilegious. Is that part of the anger?

Sorrel: Yes, that's the Punk Rock side of it. A lot of Goths play with religious symbolism, but the Gothic Movement is not a religious thing. I know Goths who are Mormon, Catholic, Wiccan, Buddhist...

Goths wear mostly black or white: the colors of death. Some women wear veils or nun's habits, signifying sexual secrecy and inaccessibility. Others wear white shrouds or wedding gowns depicting the "Bride of Death." These "children of the night" rarely appear before 11 p.m., and in some clubs religious images may be projected on the walls. Observing dancers at a Goth club is like watching an art-piece or a dance performance. Many dancers interpret the music with dramatic gestures, while others simply sway slowly to the music. Clubs have private dance areas for individuals who wish to occupy a secluded area on the dance floor with minimal physical contact with other dancers. Collisions between dancers are rare, but when they happen, apologies are infused with a Renaissance gentility. Goths value codes of chivalry as a characteristic of being well-cultured.

"Net Goths" are on the world wide web: "The Dark Web," "Black Page for a Banshee," "Closed Caskets for the Living Impaired," and "Dark Domain" are but a few sites. If you are into vampires you can commune with "Children of the Night" and "Vampires Way." They publish their own "zines" with art, poetry, bizarre dreams, and graveyard reviews. Goths love to visit graveyards. By visiting the places of the dead, and by putting on the cosmetic mask and theatrical costume of death, they are reminded that they are truly alive. Their zines tell them which graveyards are the most beautiful to visit worldwide. There they commune with the dead or simply picnic.

Colette: Do you live at home with your parents, or with other Goths?

Sorrel: I live in my home. I moved out when I was eighteen. Actually I have my own house now, and it's close to the cemetery, so that's good. That's why I wanted to live there. When I travel abroad I spend most of my time in the art museums and the cemeteries. My favorite cemetery anywhere is just outside Paris. That's where I met all my friends.

Colette: Were they Goths? So what do you do, just go in and sit on a tomb and wait for people to come in and then say, "Are you a Goth?"

Sorrel: You can tell (*laughter*). I just happened to be in the right place at the right time, this one little area in the cemetery where they go. I went to the cemetery every day for about three weeks, and I did not know anybody. Suddenly there were all these people in black, and I said, "Oh, there you are," and we were instantly friends. It's a wonderful thing, It's an instant community. It's like being part of a religious group in that sense, I suppose.

Colette: Three weeks, that's a long time for a young person to be alone in a foreign country where you do not know anyone.

Sorrel: Yes, it was a bit. In Prague I had some connections. I was there for about a week, then I came back to Paris. Yes, it was lonely. I spent all the time in the museums, so I was very happy. I was in ecstasy too, just being around all the art, being able to sketch it and live it and breathe it. It's great to travel. I think it's the best education there is.

Goths have a saying: "Every day is Halloween." Halloween is an ancient Celtic festival celebrated between the old and the new Celtic year. On that night the veil between this world and "The Otherworld" or "Dun Scaith" (Fortress of Shadows) is thinnest, and the ancestral dead can return to bring gifts to the living. Celts understand the importance of ritualizing death. Their funeral rite is called "the wake," and until recent times it was attended by professional mourners whose job it was to "keen," sing and wail in order to stimulate grief for the loss of the dead one. Only after the completion of the mourning process could the feast and celebration of life begin. The Goths remind us, like the Celts, that the time in between is important. They can be seen to be our mourners, "keening" us to grieve for all we have lost in this century, as only when this work is done should we celebrate our New Age.

Works Cited

Eliade, Mircea. *Shamanism: Archaic Techniques of Ecstasy.* Trans. William R. Trask. Bollingen Series. Princeton: Princeton UP, 1974.

Hillman, James. *The Dream and the Underworld.* New York: Harper & Row, 1979.

____________. "In Defence of Melancholy." Symposium. Pacifica Graduate Institute, Santa Barbara, California, November 7, 1992.

Johnson, R. *Ecstasy.* San Francisco: HarperSan Francisco, 1987.

Jung, C. G. "Civilization in Transition." *CW 10.* Trans. R. F. C. Hull. Princeton: Princeton UP, 1964.

Beings from Outer Space

JAMES BENNETT

The "Heaven's Gate" suicides, which took place in March 1997,[1] are understandable from a perspective as yet unrepresented in commentaries. The term "identification with an archetype"

[1] *Editors' Note*: During this event, which took place in Rancho Sante Fe, a suburb north of San Diego, thirty-nine members of a spiritual group called Heaven's Gate were found dead in the rented mansion that had been their home. They had committed suicide by swallowing apple sauce or pudding laced with phenobarbital and chased down with vodka, followed by suffocation with plastic bags. Their leader, Marshall Herff Applewhite, had taught his followers (who all had short hair and wore baggy clothes so as not to show their sexuality and to avoid lust and other earthly appetites) to prepare for a "Higher Kingdom." The group was founded in 1975, and members had lived cheaply in the house which was furnished with items from discount stores. Newspaper reports said members had supported themselves by designing websites for the Internet and were known for their efficiency and ability. The group suicide was planned to coincide with the comet Hale-Bopp's passing by close to Earth. Applewhite preached his doctrine, a strange combination of beliefs, on an Internet website in an attempt to recruit more followers. He claimed that an UFO coming from the "Next Level Above Human" was following in the slipstream of the comet and had come to take him and his followers home. This was the appointed time to shed their "containers," the word the group used for their bodies. Almost all of them were found wearing new, black Nike running sneakers and diamond shaped purple shrouds over their faces and upper bodies. Each one of the dead had packed a suitcase with clothes, notebooks, and lip-balm, with a five dollar bill and a stash of quarters in their pockets. Evidently, Applewhite and some of the other men had been castrated years before this collective suicide.

James Bennett is a psychotherapist in private practice in Arlington, Massachusetts. Originally from the United Kingdom, he has studied and worked with dreams, myth, fairy tales, and culture since 1968.

was originally used by C. G. Jung when he wrote about the dangers of encountering the world of images and symbols, what he called the Collective Unconscious, what some call the Imaginal World. While it may be true that the seekers of "Heaven's Gate" were exposed to forms of mind-control often found in such cults, I believe there is something else that accounts for, in addition to this, the intensity of attachment to their leader, and the apparent disregard and joy with which they "shed their containers."

The archetypal context of these suicides is discernible in various cultural trends of the last few years, namely the increase in stories of abductions by aliens and the widespread belief in the culture that we are regularly visited by alien spacecraft and that the government is covering this up. Part of this archetypal context is the scenario presented in the film, *Close Encounters of the Third Kind*, where Richard Dreyfus's character becomes one of the first humans to leave earth in a craft belonging to a civilization more technologically and, it appears, spiritually sophisticated than our own. We might also think to the film *E.T.*, where the stranded alien, strangely reptilian and possessed of wide-eyed innocence, longs to rejoin the ship that will take him to his planet of origin.

The "shadow" of this archetypal context is expressed in films such as *Independence Day*, where the aliens visiting earth are hostile and have as their goal the destruction of humanity and the exploitation of the planet. Even the reported abduction experiences are divided between those who describe cold, ruthless, and clinical beings who perform Nazi-style experiments on human subjects and those who talk of benign encounters with spiritual beings here to teach us about the oneness of everything and the power of love. While watching *Independence Day*, it seemed apparent that the aliens represent a projection of our darker relationship to planet earth—we are the creatures who threaten to dominate, exploit, and create a Hell here. We are confronting the Darth Vaders of our imaginings and are trying to resolve the issue of the wise use of power—or "The Force" as it is called in the *Star Wars Trilogy* (recently resurrected for a new generation).

This is linked to the "Heaven's Gate" cult and the desire to transcend the experience of embodied sensual life which was reflected in their lives and actions. What they outwardly displayed could be a yearning in the rest of us. Most of us, to one degree or another, are caught between the archetypal poles of heaven and earth, spirit and matter, up and down. We are trying to work out a way to resolve the tensions which exist between these different parts of our being and the splits which are present there by virtue of the fact that they are opposites—or at least apparently so. There is a tendency for us to deny the spiritual dimension and focus entirely on the material or to devalue the psychical realm and elevate the spiritual. Either way, there is a degrading of what it means to be human, and a loss of soul occurs.

If we are dealing with a flight from earth, a fleeing from physical, embodied experience in favor of the journey to Heaven, what is it that is going on? What we run away from we feel a strong pull towards, or we would not need to fly away. If we try to deny its hold on us, we secretly end up serving it, albeit in a distorted way. We can end up being possessed by an archetype or, to put it another way, what we repress ends up consuming us.

Consider the voluntary castration of several of the male cultists. While horrifying to our sensibilities, there are precedents for this in history. The priests of Cybele, following the example of the god Attis, castrated themselves in a religious frenzy in order to become servants of the Goddess and serve in her temple alongside her priestesses. Cybele, a Near-Eastern goddess whose worship spread to Greece and Rome from Asia Minor, is a Great Mother goddess with chthonic characteristics that include her archetypal associations with birth, sex, and death. Her name has been etymologically linked to words for crypt and cave, and she has been associated with the ancient figure of the Black Goddess, whose later forms include the Black Madonnas connected with shrines in Europe (including the most famous in Einsedeln, Switzerland). When she appeared in Rome in 204 B.C.E., one of her images was a black meteorite—the womb (space) from which matter comes. She appears to be a kind of fertility goddess.

It seems possible that the Heaven's Gate cultists, while consciously repudiating the physical realm and sexuality, were unconsciously worshipers of a Great Mother in her dark aspect and were caught up in an archetypal drama that was catalyzed by their leaders. While this may seem surprising, other details pointing to this can be found in the patchwork cosmology that their leader, Applewhite, created.

According to Applewhite the Mother Ship and its fleet, which he and his followers were to rendezvous with in the wake of the comet, had come from the core of the planet Pluto (named after the god of the

Underworld). This gives the "next-level" fleet decidedly chthonic associations. After "shedding their containers," the Heaven's Gaters were to enter the Mother Ship—which can be read as the body of the Great Mother—and return to their home in the core of Pluto. Applewhite—identified as he was with the dying/resurrecting Jesus, and thereby linking himself with a whole train of such sacrificial gods, including the self-castrator Attis whose ancient rites were celebrated between March 23 and 25 each year—chose this time frame to play out the archetypal drama. In the Cybele/Attis rituals, March 24 was known as the Day of Blood, since it was the day the self-mutilation occurred. Therefore, it is archetypally appropriate that it was during these few days that the Heaven's Gaters chose to move to their "next-level," acting out the initiatory descent into the Underworld that they were trying to fly away from.

The similarities continue. The worshippers of Cybele/Attis mutilated themselves at the foot of a sacred pine tree which had been decorated with wreaths of violets two days before. The Heaven's Gaters were found dead with purple drapes over their faces. Perhaps an uncanny echo of the ancient rites, the color was later associated with the death and resurrection of Jesus at Easter. In their state of archetypal identification, did they literalize the archetype of death and rebirth, activated as it is each year by the advent of spring (when, incidentally, the suicide rate tends to increase each year)?

What can be understood by these examples is that Heaven and Earth are a syzygy ("yoked together"). They are a pair of opposites which dance together and are woven into each other. Persons and groups who deny these images are in danger of being flooded with archetypal contents which they then act out (and vice versa). Part of the archetypal dimension of the Earth Pole of Being[2] is the tradition of the Underworld (which Christianity demonized long ago and renamed Hell), thus making people in our culture vulnerable to a kind of archetypal splitting. Traditionally, one enters the Underworld by descending into the body of the Earth—both literally (as in caves or

---

[2] There are two cosmic principles in Chinese philosophy: *Yin* and *Yang*. They are conceived of as two sides of a circle divided into light and dark, known as the *t'ai chi t'u* = the supreme ultimate. The Earth Pole of the polarity is the dark or *Yin* segment of the circle. For a discussion of this concept, see Chapter 10 of Edward Whitmont's *Return of the Goddess*. See also the *I Ching* (London: Routledge, 1950), where there is a commentary by the Confucian School which refers to the archetypal principles of Heaven and Earth. "There are no greater Primal images than heaven and earth." (319)

crypts)—or imaginally (through openings in the ground or descending into caverns) as in shamanic journeys. The suppression of the Earth Pole of Being,[3] which includes our connection to the Underworld, risks the danger that this beautiful planet we steward will become a literal Hell due to its devaluation and degradation.

Far from indulging in a kind of manic flight from our corporeal existence and then from the Earth—which is our home just as much as our home is at the level of the stars—it seems that what is required is exactly the opposite. We need to embrace our descent to inhabit our physical presence in a world (which includes our desires and attachments), and to do all this with as much awareness as we can. This is the alchemical process of transforming lead into gold or to die before you die, as the Sufis imagine it. We are cooked in the cauldron of matter. This embrace of the Earth pole of Being[4] also involves a descent into the Underworld and is an acknowledgment of the unity that exists between humans and the soul of the world. For as R. J. Stewart points out in his book, *The Underworld Initiation*, there is an ancient tradition which states that, if we go deep enough into the Underworld, we emerge among the stars. Or, following the Gnostics, we do the soul work of releasing the sparks of spirit in matter. This is to accept our role as stewards of the planet.

This descent also involves embracing our mortality, as painful as this can be. The Underworld journey is a process of shedding and stripping away as much as it is also a cauldron of renewal. It is perhaps significant that a large number of Heaven's Gaters were aged forty to fifty and older. The events which led to their deaths could be viewed as a mid-life passage. It seems they chose to literalize the death/rebirth mythos that is an integral part of the mid-life initiation, opting for a kind of premature transcendence or pseudo-resurrection rather than suffering through the confrontation with personal death that is a painful yet essential part of human experience.

[3] See Mircea Eliade, *Shamanism: Archaic Techniques of Ecstacy* (Princeton: Princeton UP, 1972). In this book Eliade describes the shaman's universe as consisting of three levels. Human beings live on the Earth in a middle world,between an upper world and a lower world (the latter two are often associated with the sky and the underworld). The three zones are usually linked by a central vertical axis,which is sometimes referred to as the *Axis Mundi* or Axis of the World.

[4] See James Hillman on the levels of "earth" in the section "Underground and Underworld," *The Dream and the Underworld.* See also Hillman on "Nature Alive" in his essay "Pan," quoted in *A Blue Fire* (Harper Perrennial, 1989).

Women, Depression, and the Soul-Image

KAREN O. HODGES

Depression is more common in women than in men, in fact, dramatically so. This observation was made as early as 1851 by French physician Jules Falret. Though most of us use the term "depression" in a vague and inclusive sense, researchers have found a variety of ways to validate this observation in recent decades using precisely defined diagnostic categories. Leaving aside the special case of depressions associated with bipolar disorder, women are now considered between 1.6 and 2 times more likely to suffer from depression than men.[1] To understand gender, its meaning

[1] Many questions have been raised about these findings. Notably, some psychologists have wondered whether women might simply be more inclined to acknowledge, to report, or to seek help for depressive symptoms. Weissman and Klerman examined such questions in their review of research on the link between gender and depression (Weissman & Klerman, 1977). They concluded that the preponderance of depression in women is real (that is, not an artifact of response bias) and that neither endocrine physiology nor any of the other possible contributing factors examined so far can be the determining factor. They characterized this phenomenon as a long-term trend, though recent evidence suggests a short-term upswing. And they considered it more or less cross-cultural, though more study is needed in non-Western countries. Another open question was whether depression in men is missed due to its being disguised by alcoholism.

Karen O. Hodges holds a doctorate in Literature and is a Jungian analyst who trained in Zürich. She has a private practice in Charlotte, North Carolina.

for the individual and how it affects one's experience in the world, this vulnerability should be taken into account.

Jung lamented that from its very beginnings psychology was inclined to reduce such matters to biology, denying that psyche is a phenomenon in its own right, with its own experience, its own efficacy, and its own responsibility for meeting the challenges of existence. Where a clear interaction can be seen to occur between psyche and soma, as in the case of what is now called melancholic depression, it is tempting to adopt such a reductive approach. Today there are antidepressant drugs which are effective in some cases. Enchanted with these drugs, popular thinking tends to repeat that depression is simply "a chemical imbalance in the brain." Yet authors like Silvano Arieti and Jules Bemporad, who have worked extensively with depression, point out that a physiological correlate does not prove a physiological cause.[2] Many cling to the hope that we can exorcise depression through technology; that we can get rid of it without getting our hands dirty, so to speak. But this is not a realistic hope.

Melancholic depression has been my special interest since I entered Jungian studies. Before that time, I worked in the field of women's health, where I had the opportunity to observe that the menstrual cycle, pregnancy, and childbirth can effect women's moods, sometimes in crippling ways. Hormones administered for birth control or for the treatment of menopausal symptoms can do the same. Yet the role of hormones in women's depression, long suspected as a factor in its high incidence, remains unclear and cannot, in any case, tell the whole story.

As a midwife's assistant attending home births, I saw how sensitive a woman's body can be to the psychological ambiance. For example, what is going on beneath the level of words between a woman giving birth and her husband can dramatically influence the course of labor, and most midwives have learned to take this factor seriously. There are few autonomous processes in the body as impressive as those at work in childbirth. The forces which expel the child from the womb have an elemental power and urgency which can be terrifying to behold, much less to experience in one's own body. Labor is a veritable

[2] These authors not only warn against reducing depression to a body phenomenon but doubt that physical symptoms of severe depression result from any specific or direct physiological mechanism. On the contrary, they tend to see depression as primarily psychological in nature (Arieti and Bemporad, 1978, 71).

juggernaut, yet it can be blocked to the point of endangering both a mother's and an infant's life if there is a psychic knot constellated in the room. When speaking of the reproductive physiology of woman, it seems that we should allow for the powerful influence of psyche on soma, as well as vice versa. If we attribute a woman's depression to "hormones," then we can be sure that her soul is involved as well.

The word "soul" belongs to any discussion of depression in a special way. If we want to look beyond "chemical imbalance in the brain" to the subjective meaning of depression, we must consider the ways in which depression has expressed itself in fantasy. Over and over again these expressions point to a broken relationship with, an inability to connect with, soul. Though many different nuances and shades of meaning adhere to it, a common thread is its link with psychic animation. It is soul that enlivens us in the sense of generating engagement with life and all the energies that flow therefrom. When engagement gives way to depression, we feel that some inner factor of importance has either abandoned us or been taken from us by malignant forces. Sometimes this factor is identified (though never quite identical) with life itself. The vegetative symptoms of severe depression seem to act out a fantasy of living death with a loss of life energy so profound that at times observers have felt they were witnessing an "imitation of death."

Jung, in reflecting upon soul as a psychological function, came to regard its connection with psychic vitality as essential; anima was, for him, "the archetype of life." In men for whom anima recedes after mid-life, Jung observed the death of spontaneity and flexibility along with loss of vitality. Their lives were dominated by weariness and resignation, for it is anima that "makes us believe incredible things, that life may be lived." Such depressive states can perhaps best be described in negative terms, then: absence of anima. What is seen is the individual's reaction to this lack, and if we look for what is behind this reaction, we find a sense of the void. One cannot help but be struck by the resemblance between loss of anima as described by Jung and the definition of melancholic depression in the *Diagnostic and Statistical Manual of Mental Disorders* (DSM-4), right down to the detail of being "somber and moody on waking."[3]

---

[3] Compare *CW 9i*, § 56, 147 to "Major Depressive Episode, Melancholic Type" in the *Diagnostic and Statistical Manual.* Jung lifted the phrase, "sombre and moody on waking," from Richard Wilhelm's translation of *The Secret of the* (*cont.*)

Of course it is not only for aging men that this fantasy of anima depletion has resonance. Consider Aaron Beck's widely accepted "cognitive triad" characterizing depression in general: negative expectations of the environment and of the future, along with negative views of one's self. Can we not understand this negativity as all that remains in the wake of receding anima? Chronically depressed persons, having lost the capacity to "believe incredible things," can only pride themselves on being realists *par excellence*, that is, capable of the most unflinching pessimism. Ideas of hope, relatedness, and meaning do belong to the imaginal world of depression but the conscious mind feels compelled to drive them back into the shadows: the impossible wish cannot be entertained. It will only cause suffering.[4] This destructive "realism" has many of the features of negative animus. Indeed, if anima plays a key role in depression, we should expect to find animus involved as well, for these two are an inseparable pair in Jung's psychology: partners in the archetypal dynamic pictured as a syzygy. Only by observing how anima and animus step into motion together, how they join the dance, can we get a feeling for what the psyche is doing in depression. Put in a different way, the fantasy of the syzygy helps us to make meaningful connections between seemingly unrelated aspects of depression.

Jung's practice of giving first importance to the fantasy of psychic states such as depression has often marked him as outside the scientific mainstream. However, there is an increasing realization that fantasy, sometimes described as "the work of culture," is so intertwined with determinate facts that it cannot be left out of the picture. Where Jung was once denigrated as "a mystic," anthropologists now criticize the naïveté of the National Institute of Mental Health in attempting to refine Western disease categories—in particular depression—for

Golden Flower, translated as, "Whoever is sombre and moody on waking...is fettered to the anima [*p'o*]" (*CW 13*, § 57).

[4] Consider the following passage from Silvano Arieti: "In...very serious cases the patient feels or acts as if he had reached an inevitable conclusion that his life is meaningless and worthless. The intense depression that accompanies this apparent conclusion actually betrays the patient's attachment to and love for life, and his inherent premise that life is meaningful and should be worthwhile... In his inner self the patient is not one of those people who consider the events of the cosmos to be due to random collisions of atoms, transformed by chance into organized unities, and completely independent from the needs of the human heart" (Arieti and Bemporad, 1978, 9).

cross-cultural use. Can we really wash out all subjectivity and understand mental illness in purely scientific terms? Will those terms not inevitably bear the stamp of Western culture? And is not mental suffering differently experienced when it is differently understood? The question has even been raised whether, when we have peeled away all layers of ethnocentricity, anything of depression remains. Psychological anthropologist Richard Shweder may have started on the right track by framing his answer not in biomedical terms but in terms of a concept found in many tribal cultures: that of soul loss.[5] Thus anthropology, even while insisting upon cultural relativism, brings us back to a fantasy of depression so basic that we may well think of it as archetypal. Given the higher rate of depression in women one might ask, then, how the experience of soul loss is different, perhaps more of an immediate threat, for women than for men?

Jung put gender in the foreground of his view of soul. In fact, he settled on the startling idea that woman may not have an anima, a "feminine" soul, at all. Rather, she is anima—that is, she not only carries anima projections for men but is the archaic origin of the projected image and therefore suited to carry it by her very nature. At the same time, Jung did not wish to depict woman's psyche as altogether unlike man's in its experience of the opposite sex. He concluded that, in spite of the asymmetries between the two in their childhood development, woman is the mirror image of man. She possesses a "masculine" soul or animus which is projected onto men. In dreams she meets her soul in masculine guise, and at the highest level of development, it is this male figure (or the function he represents) which leads her to a spiritual knowledge of self.

It remains unclear whether Jung assumed the dynamics of animus to be identical with those of anima, particularly because of his tendency to use the German term, *Seele* ("soul") for both. But English translators

[5] Understanding depression as soul loss, Shweder tends to emphasize a sense of "emptiness" as the definitive subjective experience in this state. He shows no evidence of familiarity with Jung and does not equate soul with anima but is rather making use of a familiar anthropological term. In this context soul might be defined simply as that which distinguishes living entities from non-living ones. Shweder describes this concept and ideas associated with loss of soul (soul wandering from the body in sleep and death) as "a sophisticated and nearly universal doctrine" around the world (Shweder, 1985, 193). It should be noted that Shweder includes spirit within the concept of soul. For example he treats "dispirited" and "depressed" as more or less synonymous. *Ibid.*, 198.

of Jung's *Collected Works* accentuated his insistence upon the distinct and masculine character of woman's soul by using animus as a preferred translation for *Seele* where women were under discussion.[6] What was the point that Jung hoped to make by using this masculine form in place of the feminine anima? Was he simply highlighting certain typical attributes of woman's soul as personified in dreams and fantasy: male gender, heterosexual charisma? Or was he pointing to more fundamental psychological differences between men and women?

"Animus" is a word with a broad array of meanings in the original Latin, one of them indeed being "soul." Yet we can observe, in its linguistic metamorphoses over time, a certain dwindling down until we are left with two rather narrow meanings in English today. The first equates animus with analytical thought, verbal consciousness, or *logos*. It is a definition which we owe entirely to Jung, originating in a distinction made between animus and anima by certain Roman philosophers. The second meaning is that in general usage, where animus has distinctly heroic and adversarial associations. For example *The Oxford English Dictionary* defines animus as "animating spirit or temper, usually of a hostile character." In philosophic moments, Jung made much of the *logos* character of a woman's supposedly masculine soul. But it was the ordinary English meaning, the overtone of interpersonal conflict, which seemed to catch his imagination and color the discussion of woman's soul in Jungian literature. Jung repeatedly complained of argumentative women, attributing it to animus possession, seemingly unaware of his own bias in that moment. Though acknowledging the way in which animosity between the sexes can enter a feedback loop, Jung held on to his authority to overrule the opinions of women, thus setting a precedent for possible misuse of the animus concept as a weapon for discrediting female opponents.

Jung's idea of a masculine soul or animus entails a confusion—not because masculinity cannot be soulful, but because what is heroic, willfully self-promoting, and adversarial belongs more to the world of persona than to soul. Animus not only lacks soulful qualities but, at some level, countervails them. It would not be out of keeping with Jung's understanding of animus to differentiate anima and animus as

[6] A full account of the editorial decisions involved in the translation of *Seele* and *Psyche* is given in *CW 12*, § 9, n.2.

"soul" and "spirit" respectively.[7] And, to give this point due emphasis, soul-images will be assumed here as a function of anima psychology. If a false sense of clarity on the subject is thereby created, then perhaps it will serve a compensatory function, making it a little easier for women to separate their own personal uncertainties from whatever confusion is inherent in Jung's theory.

Almost from the beginning, the Jungian school has been plagued by objections that it does not adequately represent the psychology of women. These objections often focus on the concept of negative animus, which lends itself to misogyny. A more subtle objection is related to the common (in fact, typical) appearance of animus in women's dreams and fantasies as a disturbing figure who intimidates, inspires dread, or threatens harm. We have already glimpsed the role that negative animus may play in depression in general. To this may now be added the special problems that women seem to encounter with negative animus. Far from being an image for what is lost in depression, as might be expected from Jung's equation of animus with a woman's soul-image, this figure attacks a woman's sense of self, whether as a collective-minded critic (the "committee") or in the more violent and primitive guise of the rapist.[8] He dehumanizes her, asks her to conform to cultural norms which may express an alien (masculine) point of view, and treats her as a soulless object. We might think of him as a depression-making factor—one which, in women, takes on the charismatic authority of the contrasexual.

It might seem that the key to depression in women is already in our hands. Indeed, beginning with Emma Jung, there has been a tendency for Jungian analysts to regard negative animus as a causal factor in women's depression.[9] But negative animus is rarely transformed by being put at the center of a woman's attention in analysis. On the contrary, it is anima which needs to be strengthened in the syzygy, evoked and energized by our attention. And where a woman is in the grip of depression, this is doubly so. We need to remember what tribal healers often believe about soul loss: that nothing can change for the sufferer until the soul is tracked down and retrieved, that is, until

[7] The distinction between soul and spirit is by no means universal.

[8] The fact that symbolic rape may turn out to be an important initiation for women belongs to a different train of thought than the one I am pursuing here which is limited to the phenomenology of soul loss.

[9] Emma Jung, 1957, and Alex, 1968.

connection can be reestablished. To put this in more psychological terms, wherever there is a disturbance of mood, anima is just as vitally implicated in recovery as in falling ill.

There are many situations in which good can come of a woman standing up to animus, both within and outside herself, but how can she find the vitality to do so without anima? Anima flows in the psyche as blood flows in the body: It softens, not by predisposing us to yield, but by the assurance of well-being that it brings. Accordingly, an assertion has been circulating about the Jungian world for some time now: that anima, "the archetype of life," does play an active role in the psychology of women.

The Relationship Between Woman and Anima

One of the most vivid memories I retain from my training to become a Jungian analyst in Zürich is the consternation I felt at being told that woman has no anima or feminine soul-image. This reaction was an emotional one, and I felt deeply wounded. On the one hand, Jung's fantasy of gender did not seem to fit my experience. On the other hand, I sensed that a claim to exclusive male rights in the anima mirrored social realities which are cruel in their psychological effects on women. To say that woman is destined to "be" rather than to "have" anima is much like saying that women must serve men—that they must provide erotic interest and all the services, humble as they may be, which render life more physically and psychologically accommodating for them. And women must do this without hope of being provided for in analogous ways.

The shock of this first encounter has since been mitigated by contact with authors like James Hillman, Edward Whitmont, and Verena Kast, who have revised Jung's ideas of the phenomenology of gender in significant ways. Many Jungians now acknowledge themselves to be in a certain creative tension around the concept of the soul-image, at least insofar as it concerns sexual orientation (who one loves) and social role (one's legitimate hopes and ambitions in the world of work). But shreds of the past still cling to us.

Jung was not only a doctor but a spokesman for that imaginal world in which one can ask, "*Habet mulier animam*?" ("Does woman have a soul?"). We continue to be influenced by that imagery, with its extensive and complexly interwoven strands, albeit to a lesser degree than was Jung in the 1920s and 1930s while developing his ideas about the soul-image. For the question of how a woman's experience of anima differs from that of men, awareness of this historical background leads us part way to an answer. Who among us can disentangle what we experience from the way it is imagined? And who can entirely disentangle imagination from the collective psyche? If the collective eye cannot perceive a soul in woman, then individual women will inevitably tend to be handicapped by the same blind spot.

Neither anima nor soul is a scientific term, nor should they be tortured into some shape fit for scientific discourse. Their power lies precisely in the subjective resonance they set up among interlocutors. They belong to a commonality of experience with others. To invent different names for the phenomenology of soul in women and in men is equivalent to drawing epicycles on epicycles, as astronomers once did to make the movement of the stars fit Ptolemy's outmoded picture of the cosmos. To give up the old cosmology was wrenching because it meant acknowledging that I, the observer, am not at the center. To give up Jung's gender psychology will be equally wrenching for those accustomed to an androcentric perspective. But how else are we to find the gravitational center of the psyche?[10]

To acknowledge relationship with anima as a human potential independent of gender has repercussions for woman at a practical level as well. It legitimates her pursuit of goals, her exercise of judgment, and her creativity—in short, an ego which is not in contradiction with itself, not merely a masculine structure within a female psyche. Dividing the psychic universe along lines of gender, as Jung did, cuts women off from both humanity and those cultural activities which contribute to collective consciousness, activities for which one must not just "be" but "have" anima. Oddly enough, it cuts women off from one another as well.

Many of us women can only read the *Collected Works* of Jung with a tremendous "as if" standing between ourselves and the words. We read as if we were men. How refreshing it is when someone stands up and says the obvious. When Jung spoke of women, he meant us. When he complained of "Logos" in women as "often only a regrettable

[10] Jung envisioned a similar shift that ideally takes place in mid-life, a shift of one's psychic center from ego to Self. Significantly, this is the same phase of life in which many individuals experience changes, both physical and psychological, which can be seen as perhaps a greater androgyny.

accident. ...because it consists of *opinions* instead of reflections,..."[11] he was insulting the intelligence of a great number, perhaps the majority, of his most serious readers. Jung's masculine psychology is simply the psychology of consciousness. The woman he portrayed is not quite marred by this fateful gift nor disturbed by the creative conflicts it brings in its wake. In short, she is not quite human.

The question of whether modern, educated women participate in *logos* or analytical consciousness at the same level as men is relevant to the issue at hand. For human consciousness always comes into being through a kind of split in the psyche. Reflection stands over against the phenomenon of life. Where consciousness is established, how could anima (the archetype of life) not be constellated as a more or less autonomous function, in women as well as in men? Individuals differ in the degree to which their consciousness has developed a detached, "solar" quality, but even by moonlight, no one sees far into anima. It is in the nature of anima to present itself through projections. And a woman, as well as a man, may develop a conscious relationship with soul through those projections.

This having been said, it is important to acknowledge that Western culture preferentially encourages the anima projections of males. It provides men with an abundance of stimulating fantasy material which is theirs to explore and to play with. (Do men ever have to read books as if they were women?) Its institutions—particularly that of marriage—support men's anima projections onto women. No discussion of gender differences in depression is complete without mentioning studies demonstrating the protective effect of marriage for men, alongside the fact that marriage puts women at psychological risk.[12] The fact is that single, divorced, and widowed women all have lower rates of mental illness, including depression, than those who are married, whereas the picture is exactly reversed for men.

---

[11] *CW 9ii*, § 29. *Editors' note*: The Jung quote without the ellipsis points, which seems interesting in light of this essay's argument, reads: "This is because it consists of *opinions* instead of reflections, and by opinions I mean *a priori* assumptions that lay claim to absolute truth."

[12] In addition to the original findings to this effect made by W. R. Gove in 1972, Weissman and Klerman (1977, 106) cite subsequent confirmation by additional studies.

Asexual Projections of Anima

Much of our difficulty with the concept of anima in women may be related to an old fantasy of soul. Here, the term "fantasy" can be defined as a projection which, like all projections, begins as something natural, spontaneous, and unintended: the process of finding an image for what is hidden in the darkness of psychic subjectivity. Our projections are precious elements in the life of the imagination for they create the reflective surface in which our nature may be seen. How then do we project anima? It seems that, for many males, this projection catches up the sexual instinct in a powerful way. The situation tends to be more complex for women.

Jung was fond of pointing to personifications of anima in art and literature as confirmation of his idea that this figure is a function of male heterosexuality. Consider the experience of poets in the Western tradition whose psychological process may be understood as a derivative of anima (the Muse). That sexual feeling drives this process is often proclaimed in the poems themselves. If not, it may be reflected indirectly in their motifs and images, or it may lie hidden in the poet's biography. But over and over again, sexuality is the way by which the poet comes into contact with anima and gains its powers for himself. At the same time it is striking how often attainment of the desired woman remains out of the poet's reach. We could go so far as to say that no woman carrying potent anima projections for the poet should ever be comfortably possessed. The mundane, biological, and social aspect of the quest must be thwarted in some measure so as not to extinguish the psychic or soul element. The lyric tradition in the Western world, from Sappho to Yeats to the present moment, has been indelibly marked by this dynamic and by the tragic biographies resulting from it.

However, looked at from the perspective of the work, there is no tragedy. The Muse is both like and not like that image of desire; that woman whom the poet has met in the everyday world. The potency of the image consists in the fact that it is a metaphor for something unseen which cannot be possessed. And in that sense, like all metaphor, the image brings with it a necessary tension. Where there is no paradox of like and not-like, metaphor collapses, and one no longer perceives nuance and complexity in the elements it has brought together. In fact they have been robbed of the very *principium individuationis* which makes them separate elements and which poetry celebrates as the hallmark of the real.

For example, this is what happens when imagistic language is yoked to a social or religious agenda, imbuing its ideals with the memorable and compelling qualities necessary to command allegiance: a metaphor's fullest meaning is not opened up until it is deconstructed. But to deconstruct an ideal is to weaken and perhaps destroy it. One should always, as nearly as possible, be like the ideal. What positive justification can there be for falling short (being not-like)? For example both masculine and feminine principles may be social ideals imagistically portrayed. Why would we use the same root to speak of the principle (*fem-inine*) as the person (*fem-ale*) unless we wished to express the requirement that women conform to and express "the feminine." In the post-Jungian world, much energy has been expended in making a distinction between the feminine and females (actual women), yet this distinction never quite sticks. Should we be surprised that identification between the two keeps coming back? The language itself is working against us.

Allegiance to the feminine principle is undergoing a renaissance today. Passionate and invigorated by a sense of novelty, its devotees are focused upon social reform and the remaking of culture. But they seem less content to locate the feminine principle in the socio-political realm than they are inclined to follow Jung's example, assigning it to a higher ontological level. Much as Plato's Forms were believed to underlie all phenomena, much as the double helix of DNA is seen today as the blueprint for human development, the feminine principle is regarded as the essence of being a woman. In short it defines her nature. And because living in harmony with one's nature was a primary value for Jung (close to a religious obligation), his psychology leaves little room for individual women to deviate from the feminine. Jung himself tended to speak of such deviation as a risky business, tantamount to the ego going off on some willful tangent of its own and inviting neurosis. Yet without deviation (the not-like), the paradox at the core of being human slips out of our grasp, and we are prevented from seeing women as they are, their nuance and complexity. Again, it is the *principium individuationis* that is washed out of the picture.

Now let us return to the practice of poetry in which Jung saw his anima psychology confirmed. The practice of yoking imagistic language to a social or religious agenda is generally resented as an obstacle to creativity. Poetry in particular has a subversive edge which is at times regarded as a threat to the social order, at other times afforded protection as a valuable neutral zone where freedom can safely be enjoyed. Yet poets are no different from anyone else in that their vocational role is imagined within a social context, not separate from other aspects of collective life. And ironically, it was a poet, Robert Graves, that popularized the idea that women must "be" anima rather than "have" a Muse in whose service she labors. In fact, Graves went so far as to suggest that neither male homosexuals nor women can be true poets because of the feminine and erotic character of the Muse.[13]

Graves' view of the Muse makes a larger claim: he saw her as a transcendent factor and one whose drama is enacted in the poet's personal life and vocation. In a sense, Jung saw it in reverse, characterizing the collective soul-image of the Western world as feminine, not because Anima (or Muse) is a goddess, but as a consequence of the masculine psychology peculiar to his culture. But by linking soul-image to sexuality and gender identity, Jung went down the same road as Robert Graves. He drew the conclusion that, because anima has so often been projected onto sexually desired women, this is the only legitimate form in which it can be projected. And this creates for women poets, as for all creative women, a problem which may be partly artificial, partly real: the Muse must be reckoned with.

---

[13] Robert Graves, 1948/1966, 446. On this and the following page Graves writes, "However, woman is not a poet: she is either a Muse or she is nothing." He then adds: "This is not to say that a woman should refrain from writing poems; only, that she should write as a woman, [i.e., a Muse], not as if she were an honorary man." While its meaning is not clear, the passage is remarkable for its quixotic insistence on heterosexism (we are not to believe the slander that Sappho was a lesbian) and presents a precedent for Jung's idea of the *femme inspiratrice.* Concerning the place of women and homosexual men in the ranks of poets, Peter Russell is both more generous and more faithful to the facts. He allows for lesbian feeling for a female Muse, on a par with his own. And writing on certain lyrics linked with the Islamic tradition of courtly love, he finds significance in images of the *saqi* or wine-pourer, the beautiful boy who brings together two poetic images associated with spiritual Wisdom in that tradition: that of Wine and that of the Beloved—in this case, a male anima or Muse (Russell, 1991, 56).

Consider the fact that poets today still speak of the Muse with little or no irony. A literary sensibility, more than any other, should be put off by the musty and dated quality of this expression. It must name a vital function if we are willing to limp along with it until something better comes along. The truth is that one has to "be in the mood" for creative work, and Jung tells us that mood is the specialty of the anima—not to speak of the need for a "feminine" *pied-a-terre* while one is lost in the imaginal world. But why bind anima in such a gratuitously literal-minded fashion to the image of the sexual partner? Far from being present in all cultures, this idea goes against the wisdom of many religious traditions, which see it as more of a danger than a *desideratum*. It seems important, and not only for women, to loosen the hold that this image has on the Western imagination.

In what visible forms can a heterosexual woman meet that hidden soul factor which is at work both in the world and in her own psyche? In fact poetry is full of diverse examples of such projections. We might even characterize poetry as a whole—both the process of writing and its product—as an anima "field."[14] Poetry calls anima into being with its every gesture. And the poem itself, weaving together images of the world which capture its paradoxical nature, becomes a "space between" where anima may reside. At the same time, to be moved by such images is to be drawn into life. And this is the primary function of anima in personal psychology.

But is it only through specialized cultural activities like poetry that woman can step free of the expectation that she "be" rather than "have" anima? Is the artistic or literary woman an anomaly? Quite apart from questions of gender, poets themselves have been concerned to understand their creative processes as reflective of human psychology. The Romantic poets of eighteenth century England were especially driven to psychological reflection, feeling themselves marginalized within an increasingly rational and materialistic culture, and it is these authors, more than Jung, that may help us understand anima projection. For example consider William Wordsworth's account, in the long autobiographical poem, *The Prelude*, of how he came to find creative inspiration (anima) in Nature. What he is describing, or

[14] Robert Graves considered poetry practically unique in contemporary life as a culture of anima, not only preserving but actively carrying on archaic traditions once associated with "the Triple Goddess."

imagining, is a favorable early experience of attachment with his mother, followed by a gradual transference of those feelings to nature.

> ...Blest the infant Babe,
> (For with my best conjecture I would trace
> Our Being's earthly progress,) blest the Babe,
> Nursed in his Mother's arms, who sinks to sleep
> Rocked on his Mother's breast; who with his soul
> Drinks in the feelings of his Mother's eye!
> For him, in one dear Presence, there exists
> A virtue which irradiates and exalts
> Objects through widest intercourse of sense.
> No outcast he, bewildered and depressed:
> Along his infant veins are interfused
> The gravitation and the filial bond
> Of nature that connect him with the world.[15]

Half submerged within this passage is an understanding of the nature of projection: Wordsworth seems to be speaking of projection in general in terms of the "irradiation" of objects. And behind this process one can sense the numinous presence of an *anima mundi*: Wordsworth's poetry leaves little doubt that such a transpersonal factor is involved. Nevertheless, he anticipates Jung's own insistence on linking this factor with personal psychology, placing it in the context of a developmental process set in motion by relationship with the mother. "The Babe" does not simply gaze at a mother who catches his anima projections, but rather he gains the capacity to project anima from her, first being filled with "the feelings of his Mother's eye," then participating in its "virtue." This can be understood in a concrete way: Young children become involved in what interests the mother. But, designating this field of interest simply as "the world," Wordsworth suggests a more global process. The child has learned to perceive as the mother does, that is, he perceives in a connected way.

Not only is this process felt to originate with the mother, but the "Babe" appears to be its first object, passively receiving projections as he "sinks to sleep." The mother's gaze puts something into him which is as soothing and strengthening as milk, namely, the feeling, not only of being loved but of being connected and belonging in the world. Most parents will recognize this experience from the other side of the dyad. Anyone who has looked at an infant and been

[15] Wordsworth, 1805/1857, 505 (ll. 232-244).

moved by the sense of a personality *in nuce* knows the instinctive tendency to project magical qualities onto the infant, long before much of his or her own reality can be expressed. Particularly if it is my own child, what others might see as an unprepossessing little object is "irradiated and exalted" by my fantasy—that is, ensoulled and inflated.

Folded into these lines from Wordsworth, then, is a psychology of anima projection as a capacity passed down from one generation to the next. Before it is given out, so to speak, in acts of perceiving or imagining soul outside one's self, it must be taken in as a kind of love that stimulates the sense of having a soul. Projection of soul onto the infant becomes the hinge upon which this intergenerational process turns. The woman who cannot generate projections of this kind will not be able to fulfill her time-honored role of receiving her infant into the human family.

Perhaps it is because Wordsworth lost his mother at the early age of eight that his sense of anima was not erotically focused upon a particular image of woman. However, it would not be accurate to say that Wordsworth deviated significantly from the masculine psychology of his day. At most we might point out his strong tendency towards animism, a kind of throwback to the psychology of both men and women in the tribal world. From an early age, he was deeply attached to "Nature" and predisposed to experience it as coming alive in unusual ways, personifying itself, fluid and intentional like a living being.[16] Though a similar diffuse attachment to the natural world can be felt in Jung's feeling for his Bollingen retreat, he was prone to denigrate it under the heading of *participation mystique*, a phrase implying unconsciousness and a poorly formed individual identity. Yet *participation mystique* is only one element in attachment phenomena, and it might be characterized as the starting point. The work of developmental psychologists such as Rene Spitz helps us to understand the aim or endpoint of attachment, at least for young children, in terms of psychic stimulation (animation): the energizing of mind and feeling, the awakening of curiosity and will. In Wordsworth's poem as well, the sense of connectedness felt by the sleeping "Babe" lays the groundwork for his later waking up to the world. "Widest intercourse of sense" implies attention at its most alert.

[16] Erich Neumann describes how children deprived of adequate mothering may form an attachment to the natural environment in her place (Neumann, 1990, 80).

For the archaic man and woman, lifelong attachment to the natural environment was not an indulgence of primal unconsciousness. On the contrary, it sharpened powers of observation and discrimination required by their everyday existence. We today pay a heavy price for our bias against animism, that is, projection of soul into the nonhuman sphere. Perceiving the world without this aliveness, we have apparently lost the capacity to live in equilibrium with our environment.[17]

Much of our understanding of attachment phenomena has evolved since Jung's ideas were formed. Moreover, there was a blind spot in Jung's thinking about women's relationships with their children which left a great gap in his understanding of their eros. It seems important, then, to round out the image of the mother given us by Wordsworth in "The Prelude" with detail of a more mundane kind, so that the anima of women can be seen. For example consider the colloquial expression, "baby lust," a term sometimes used by women to describe that powerful longing which may be sparked by seeing a charming baby or another woman with her infant in arms.[18] Naturally it would be impossible to use this expression as casually as we do if it were literally a matter of genital sexuality. Instead the phrase plays on something that current infant research affirms—that here is a form of eros as passionate and highly focused as any sexual feeling yet not subject to the incest taboo. Indeed the eros of motherhood needs to be a driving force capable of overriding ego because of the demands made by the mothering role.

"Baby lust" may give rise to projections just as troublesome as sexual obsession, sabotaging a woman's plans for the future (e.g. contraceptive intentions) or leading to a loss of self in preoccupation with the child. Yet just as with sexual projections, our lives may feel empty without such experiences. The child whose birth carries so

[17] The Romantic feeling for Nature has been ridiculed as regressive. In fact, while some Romantic poets (including Wordsworth) were able to contact what they felt to be soul inherent in the natural world, others (notably Coleridge) only grieved its absence. But in both this concern went hand in hand with an ecological awareness and accompanying ethical sensibility that were far ahead of the times.

[18] I do not wish to imply that all women experience "baby lust" or that its absence in a woman is unnatural. Nor do I wish to exclude the possibility that infants and young children carry anima projections for males, a dynamic which is perhaps more characteristic of tribal than industrialized cultures. Acknowledging that the projection of anima is a form of love, we are reminded that it can be neither forced nor reliably predicted.

much meaning for its parents may, once arrived, give as much as, perhaps more than, it receives.

Jung believed that women naturally accommodate themselves to monogamy with greater ease than men, and he looked to a difference between the souls of women and men, between anima and animus, to explain this. In the end he framed it in terms of a simplicity in woman that allows her to project her soul onto one man and to live for him. Can he not have noticed what an enormous investment of libido goes into pregnancy, childbirth, and the ongoing tasks of childcare?[19] Particularly during the first months of infancy (the nursing period), women often feel torn in two by the sexual demands of their husbands, not only because they are exhausted by the work of caring for another human being day and night, but because their eros is going to the child. It is not rare for women to long for an unborn child before finding a male partner, and providing for one's children commonly becomes the most compelling reason to preserve a marital relationship. The more insecure the economic position of women, particularly in times and places where reliable birth control is not available, the more marriage fulfills a purpose for them. Following one's heart in the choice of a mate has often been a luxury women could not afford. Even today, many women remain married to partners with whom they have unresolvable differences because they hesitate to take up the burden of single parenting. A man must be found who will provide, regardless of how easy or difficult he is to love.

Now what becomes of this attachment to the child which is so passionate and which asks so much of a woman? For the child, a favorable experience of attachment leads to separation. Is it different for the mother? Must she not also go through a process of letting go—perhaps not all at once at some fixed endpoint but over and over again with each new development that changes the child, making him or her someone new who must be met in a new way? Not only must a mother find ways to accept these developments, which are out of her control and may well bring suffering, but her capacity for relatedness must be protected in the process. Shutting down emotionally

[19] Jung mentioned the pathological situation of the woman who wants a husband only to breed her children but unaccountably omitted the normal involvement of mothers with their children or the sense of abandonment frequently experienced by their male partners as a result.

hurts a woman as much as it disables her for her mothering role, where the relationship with one child may be followed by a next and a next. Moreover, this role has a way of evolving into one of emotional responsibility for all the members of one's family, including relatives on the husband's side of the family.

Much has been said about the diffuseness of a woman's eros. Woman's biologically determined sexual responses have been characterized in this way, with the psychological equivalent portrayed as derivative. But might not the diffuseness of a woman's interest in and attachment to many different family members be seen in the context I am describing?—a viable adaptation to the typical conditions of being wife and mother in a traditional setting. As the boy Wordsworth survived the loss of his mother by finding anima in all of Nature, a woman too may survive her many "losses" by finding a larger resonance in the family, however that is embodied for her. But we can go much farther and recognize in many women a predisposition towards animism much like Wordsworth's: a contemporary animism, largely unsupported by cultural institutions, lived in terms of spontaneous feeling for one's home, one's garden, or the entire natural world.[20] The same *participation mystique* women enter to communicate with their young children provides them access to "the filial bond of nature."

This brings us back to Jung's prejudice against *participation mystique* as a sign of deficient consciousness, for though he confessed to having little insight into the domain of mother and child, Jung did take notice of the diffuseness of feeling and perception that supports woman's traditional role as protector of the family's coherence. It was this observation that enabled Jung to resolve his puzzlement over alchemy's identification of consciousness with "masculinity" (solar qualities of clarity and focus). Therefore, reluctant to stray from the world of alchemists, Jung came to think of a woman's consciousness as lunar:

[20] Marie-Louise von Franz was interested in the ideas of Heinrich Hediger, a Professor of Zoology at Zürich University, who derived territoriality in animals from the young animal's attachment to the mother's body. She went on to say that "Women, especially, suffer tremendously when they lose their territory,..." that is, their specific point of attachment to the natural environment (von Franz, 1970, 55, 56). *Editors' note*: The above von Franz quote's ellipsis points replace the following: "which is why Jung once said that he felt sorry for American women because of the moving from one place to another which is usual for them."

> It needs a very moon-like consciousness indeed to hold a large family together regardless of all the differences, and to talk and act in such a way that the harmonious relation of the parts to the whole is not only not disturbed but is actually enhanced. And where the ditch is too deep, a ray of moonlight smooths it over.[21]

Notice that though the feminine is given a kind of situational definition, Jung is trying to get at what makes women women; their very thought processes. We can hear some of his bias against this synthetic style of thinking and imagining as one that washes out individual difference, sacrificing it to the need for collective harmony. By contrast, the "masculine" capacity to achieve focus brings out conflict and individuality, and presumably shows us more of things as they are.

But this is not the only way in which individuality can be understood. The poet Robert Frost gives us an image which captures much more a life constrained by multiple relationships, a life in which individuality is realized through limitation. The image appears in the sonnet, "The Silken Tent," a portrait of Frost's friend, Kay Morrison.

> She is as in a field a silken tent
> At midday when a sunny summer breeze
> Has dried the dew and all its ropes relent,
> So that in guys it gently sways at ease,
> And its supporting central cedar pole,
> That is its pinnacle to heavenward
> And signifies the sureness of the soul,
> Seems to owe naught to any single cord,
> But strictly held by none, is loosely bound
> By countless silken ties of love and thought
> To everything on earth the compass round,
> And only by one's going slightly taut
> in the capriciousness of summer air
> Is of the slightest bondage made aware.[22]

Frost's poem shows that personality is rounded out by attachment or a multiplicity of attachments: "countless silken ties of love and thought to everything on earth the compass round." This gives the subject her "sureness of the soul," and it enables her to balance over her own center of gravity rather than dependently to lean on relationships.

---

[21] *CW 14*, § 227.

[22] Frost, 1949, 443.

The image of the silken tent is a beautiful one and, on good days, women can be like that. But the not-like must be shown as well. For, as women's vulnerability to depression demonstrates, we do not always experience "sureness of the soul." Women are also subject to a depletion of anima. To demand of woman that she match Frost's image, to demand that she never be other than strong and uncomplaining in her bondage, would be to fall into an infantile fantasy of Mother as omnipotent and all-providing—that is, a goddess and not a human being with the same psychology as males with analogous needs and desires. The curious impersonality of Frost's image gives us a clue that he inhabited the same mental universe as Jung. Woman is the silken tent; she is anima. As such she is both prettified and distanced, qualities favored in Victorian representations of the feminine ideal. But no amount of opalescent sheen (moon or silk) can disguise the fact that this woman is not seen as a person. Rather she is pictured as an inexhaustible resource. Woman's vulnerability to depression shatters this illusion if we allow it to touch us and to penetrate our fantasy of the feminine.

At some level we may all feel the old fantasy of woman as the omnipotent Mother breaking down. One can even read in *Time* magazine that "the suburbs have been particularly hard on women with young children. In the typical hunter-gatherer village, mothers can reconcile a home-life with a work life fairly gracefully, and in a richly social context." It would probably be more accurate to say that, in the hunter-gatherer village, home life and work life have not yet been so split. They are more nearly one in the culture itself. But ours is increasingly a society in which the whole cloth of life is cut and woman in her traditional role is confined to a narrower and narrower preserve—cut off from sources of renewal. A discontinuity exists between the life of soul, which is delegated to woman-as-nurturer, and the world of social intercourse.

We think we can retire to our homes to make use of soul protectively enshrined there. But soul lives in imaginative processes which seek to broaden our horizons in adulthood, renewing us through experiences, different configurations of relationship, greater challenges. If we do not support these processes, soul dries up. Woman, historically, has cushioned the effects of this drought by carrying projections of soul. But who stands between woman and the impoverishment of our culture?

Recovery of Woman's Lost Soul

Clinical depression has been linked to loss of attachment figures early in life and carries the implicit sense of something once ours that is no longer available. As Wordsworth's example suggests, a capacity for anima projection protects us from excessive grieving at the loss of attachment figures, as it protects us from shutting down to avoid further suffering. Yet depression, in which anima projection dries up and we experience both self and world as soulless, afflicts imaginative as well as unimaginative individuals. The capacity for anima projection is neither a fixed structure nor a skill that can be mechanically acquired, to be reliably available to us ever after. It is nevertheless possible to speak of a personality which knows soul and tends to be resilient, resourceful and creative in stalking it. Jung's therapeutic approach embodies, perhaps more than any other insight, his discovery that imaginative process can be educated; its development can be facilitated within an analysis.

Jung spoke of anima projection in men as both an outgrowth of attachment to the mother and a genuine shift away from it in the direction of a broader life. A similar shift in women is perceptible as the female child's focus on mother gives way to new attachments. These new attachments may reproduce the same focused and compelling quality of the original mother/infant dyad but with the element of growing-toward-separation now implicitly included. How differences between men and women contribute to their comfort or discomfort with monogamy is unclear, but if the stereotype has it that men's anima projections proliferate through sexual interest, then women can be equally expansive in their emotional investment in growing families. Paradoxically, this means being confronted again and again with the challenge of separation. Men, by contrast, are asked to look and behave as if they had moved beyond attachment, yet they are compensated by control and security in marriage. The original fantasy behind this institution was that woman can be conveyed from father to husband as property. A woman is faulted, and rightly so, for not allowing those she loves to grow beyond her. But the carrier of a man's anima can, as far as patriarchal law and custom reach, belong to him.

In effect, this means that women are expected to embody anima values such as beauty, relatedness, and emotional generosity in an atmosphere which is not conducive to any of those things. Over the centuries, women have been able to draw on certain resources which seem less important to men, such as daily intimacy with familiar people and attachment to a relatively stable home place where one's creativity can be expressed. But with industrialization, it becomes less and less possible to rely on such resources. Women now have more freedom to refuse the patriarchal arrangement, but this may lead to an even keener awareness of being emptied or depleted of soul. We are experiencing a general malaise of the psyche, in which consciousness and anima are excessively split off from one another. Until new forces are set in motion to compensate that split, it is likely that more women than men will realize it as a personal experience, a personal suffering.

Meanwhile, many of us labor under unmet needs of a highly irrational kind, needs that cannot be explained or understood without a feeling for soul as a phenomenon in its own right. That many individuals have developed such a feeling is hopeful but not enough. As long as we are caught collectively in the present bias towards engineering solutions, healing measures remain beyond our capacity collectively to imagine, and therefore, out of reach.

One of Jung's greatest contributions to psychotherapy was the realization that rationality and strenuous effort can only take us so far. In other words, the heroic attitude described here as characteristic of the animus is not appropriate for all situations, and it is especially inadequate where one's connection with the unconscious is faltering or has become negatively polarized. Jung left no doubt that the aging man who has fallen into mid-life doldrums cannot help himself by the same kind of active, driving, goal-oriented approach that might have led to his success in the business world. He must turn to his anima, not in passive surrender, but with a receptive attitude. The idea that one must "go into depression" rather than fight it has become something like dogma in Jungian circles.

All the same, Jung's ideas concerning feminine psychology seem to point depressed women in the opposite direction, along the path of intellectual discipline, reflection and discernment—in other words, the mobilization of positive animus. This fantasy of positive animus as a kind of savior for women is quite in keeping with popular ideas, not only about psychotherapy, but also about social betterment for women. There are situations in which individuation calls for, even requires, an heroic attitude. Integration of animus enables a woman to take a protective role in relation to her soul, perhaps even to calm or restrain the savage negativity that can constellate in depression.[23] But exhortations to transform the animus are a good bit more plentiful than ideas about how to do this. I have already stated my conviction that it is a strengthening and energizing of anima, not animus, that ultimately softens conflict within a syzygy.

A depression of any magnitude leaves us without energy for a fight. This is no time for heroism, for women anymore than for men. One sometimes gets the impression that the animus of depression does not need improvement so much as defeat, so that one may be allowed to collapse in peace. Clinical depressions are characterized by a natural cycle in which, as in certain kinds of infections, the disease tends to exhaust itself, and recovery can be expected to proceed in its own time. Even a well-educated, well-intentioned animus can make this into a more violent and protracted process than it needs to be.

Letting go in depression may be much like letting go in childbirth, though inestimably more difficult. It is more difficult because animus carries the logos function and therefore the capacity for perceiving meaning in one's life. A woman experiences loss of her normal sense of bodily coherence during childbirth, but she may be able to accept this for the sake of holding the baby in her arms. A person in severe depression may experience the loss of all sense of meaning, with no image whatsoever of what good might come of it. Both psychotherapy and religion attempt to provide such an image, but the paradox is that we cannot open ourselves to an experience of meaninglessness if we cling to conventional assurances. Meanwhile, in depression as in childbirth, to resist the process, to retard it, may prove fatal.

---

[23] Warren Steinberg questions whether Jung's more or less anima-oriented approach is adequate for depressions where fantasy life has gotten stuck in negativity, whether in women or in men. He calls for a mode of treatment which is not only analytical but also insistent in its demands that the patient develop greater separateness, frustrating his or her presumed predisposition to dependency (Steinberg, 1989).

Works Cited

Alex, William. "Depression in Women." Unpublished manuscript, 1968.

Arieti, Silvano and Bemporad, Jules. *Severe and Mild Depression: The Psychotherapeutic Approach.* New York: Basic Books, 1978.

Frost, Robert. *Complete Poems.* New York: Holt, Rinehart & Winston, 1949.

Graves, Robert. *The White Goddess: A Historical Grammar of Poetic Myth.* New York: Farrar, Straus & Giroux, 1948; revised ed., 1966).

Harris, Joel Chandler. *Uncle Remus: His Songs and His Sayings.* New York: Dunlap, rev. ed., 1980.

Hesiod, *Theogony & Works and Days.* Trans. M. L. West. New York: Oxford UP, 1988.

Hill, Gareth S. *Masculine and Feminine: The Natural Flow of Opposites in the Psyche.* Boston: Shambhala, 1992.

Jung, C. G. *The Collected Works.* Trans. R. F. C. Hull. Vols. 7, 9i, 9ii, 12, 13, & 14. Bollingen Series. Princeton: Princeton UP.

Jung, Emma. *Animus and Anima.* Dallas: Spring Publications, 1957; rpt. 1981.

Neumann, Erich. *The Child.* Trans. Ralph Manheim. Boston: Shambhala, 1990.

Russell, Peter. "The Figure of Woman in Islamic and Christian Love Poetry of the Middle Ages." Unpublished manuscript (copyrighted), 1991.

Samuels, Andrew. *The Plural Psyche: Personality, Morality, and the Father.* London: Routledge, 1989.

Shweder, Richard A. "Menstrual Pollution, Soul Loss, and the Comparative Study of Emotions." Eds. Arthur Kleinman and Byron Good. *Culture and Depression: Studies in the Anthropology and Cross-Cultural Psychiatry of Affect and Disorder.* Berkeley: University of California Press, 1985, 182-215.

Steinberg, Warren. "Depression: A Discussion of Jung's Ideas." *Journal of Analytical Psychology*, (34), 1989, 339-352.

Time Magazine, 54. August 28, 1995. No author stated.

von Franz, Marie-Louise. *Interpretation of Fairytales.* Dallas: Spring Publications, 1970.

Weissman Myrna M. and Klerman, Gerald L. "Sex Differences and the Epidemiology of Depression." *Arch. Gen. Psychiatry*, (34), 1977, 98-111.

Wordsworth, William. *Poetical Works.* London: Oxford UP, 1936.

Lost Souls in the Wars of the World

EDWARD TICK

He tries to read but the sentences do not hold together. He opens letters left lying on his desk for weeks, then tears them into shreds before completing them. He chain smokes. The light of the sun or a bulb burns his eyes. He does not wash. He does not fraternize. He neither cleans his room nor leaves it. He cannot stop trembling. He feels "his mind dislodge itself and teeter, like insecure luggage on an overhead rack." He squeezes his temples and holds on tightly. His friend, whose sister is majoring in psychology, delivers this word from home: "She says nobody gets a nervous breakdown from the war and all."[1] This is J. D. Salinger's fictionalized portrait of a traumatized combat soldier in Europe shortly after World War II. It is emblematic of two factors: the psyche's response to extreme violence, and the civilian public's denial of the cost to soul of such violence.

What happens when the soul experiences powers far beyond its own, overwhelming it, and attempting to dislodge it from its existence?

[1] J. D. Salinger, "For Esmé—With Love and Squalor," *Nine Stories* (New York: Bantam, 1971).

Edward Tick is a psychotherapist, lecturer, and writer who lives in Albany, New York. He specializes in treating veterans who suffer from Post-traumatic Stress Disorder and is completing a book on Asklepios.

What happens when soul experiences the physical powers unleashed by war that attempt to dislodge it by all its roots—physical, psychological, cultural, ethical, and spiritual? If "all things compose and decompose, generate and degenerate into soul," as writes James Hillman,[2] then what happens when it is only the decomposition and degeneration processes to which soul is exposed—overexposed—until it seems that is all that remains of the organic movement of life? What happens when its ecology becomes a complete Hell—bent on devastation—where the remaining good is the attempt to survive and even that attempt necessitates the doing of harm to others?

Lest it be argued that Salinger's portrait has no basis in fact, take this example of a Bosnian concentration camp survivor currently in psychotherapy, which demonstrates how a soul becomes lost during exposure to extreme violence and how a soul remains lost long after the violence has ceased:

> Ramiz, a recent immigrant to this country and a political refugee, is a Bosnian Muslim who was interred in Serbian concentration camps for almost a year. He chain smokes. He can't sleep, or when he does, he has nightmares of camp experiences. He can't concentrate enough to read or write. He avoids his wife and family and has no friends. During the day he hides in his apartment, which he cannot clean. He hides from the light. He spends hundreds of nighttime hours aimlessly walking the streets of the foreign city that hosts him or sitting in front of a television set watching programs he cannot understand. He quickly flicks off any pictures of violence. He is tortured by headaches from which he can find no relief. He rarely changes his clothes and keeps his hair cropped to the scalp as it was in the camps. He does not talk about his camp experiences. His wife and relatives say, "Nothing that can happen is terrible enough to make a person like this. He must be crazy."

This story illustrates the condition we have come to call Post-traumatic Stress Disorder. The root of this disorder lies in the brutality done to the soul which has chased soul from its connections to this world. In Post-traumatic Stress Disorder, the soul has fled the body and world, and it will not return if this condition is not recognized and directly

[2] James Hillman, *The Dream and the Underworld* (New York: Harper and Row, 1979), 26-7.

addressed.[3] Many traditional psychological workers either know little about conditions of soul or deny that extreme violence perpetrated on the adult personality can have such extensive and debilitating consequences. This gap in understanding is caused by the dominance of developmental theories of psychology which do not allow that the psyche can be affected by events experienced during the adult years.

Combat veterans have suffered from this lack of understanding. Jack, a reconnaissance patrol sergeant in Vietnam, is a good example. Dissatisfied with the psychotherapy he received from his Veterans Administration hospital, he complained that his therapist seemed to ignore what happened to him during his war experience.

> They place too much emphasis on what happened in childhood… Not that my childhood doesn't affect me. But they always steer me away from the war, as if its effects were only repeats of my childhood rather than problems in themselves. [But] I say, 'Doc, if you had 70 near fatal car accidents in one year of your life between ages 18 and 19, do you think that would mess you up all by itself?[4]

Comments such as these have been repeated with painful regularity during the two decades I have worked with combat veterans and other survivors of modern war. A great many war survivors feel themselves adrift like the debris of history in the midst of a society that "doesn't get it" because they have not personally experienced the overwhelming destruction and horror of war. Survivors feel shaken and fragmented by the exposure to such horror. They often feel utterly alone in a business-as-usual world that denies their suffering by not seeing it or blaming it on their inadequacies to "deal with it." The result is devastating: veterans feel wounded and fragmented in their essence, dislodged from the universe, and homeless in the world.

"My Soul Has Fled"

When bullets are flying or bombs are falling, when human beings by the dozens, hundreds, or even thousands, armed with killing machines, are arrayed against you, when all that you perceive appears

---

[3] See Edward Tick, "The Vietnam War and the American Shadow," *Spring 62*, 1997, for a more extensive archetypal approach to Post-traumatic Stress Disorder.

[4] Edward Tick, *Sacred Mountain: Encounters with the Vietnam Beast* (Santa Fe: Moon Bear Press, 1979), 90.

bent on your destruction, the soul responds with such terror that it simultaneously attempts to leave the world and do everything in its power to preserve its existence. Sometimes the soul becomes lost slowly, in a process of erosion due to repeated exposure to violence. Sometimes it occurs suddenly during one unexpectedly brutal event. Often survivors can recover the event, and the recovery of this memory is a critical component of psychotherapy.[5]

Gary, a Vietnam veteran, recalled vividly (and, uncharacteristically, during our first psychotherapy session), his experience of soul erosion and loss during combat. He burst into my office wearing a black leather riding jacket, tight jeans, and high black boots. He, too, cropped his hair like a concentration camp inmate. I put out my hand and introduced myself. He stared at it and grunted, "Uh huh!" He proceeded to stomp through my office, looking out each window in the waiting room, hallway, therapy room, and behind each closed door. When we entered the therapy room, he moved a chair into a corner from which he could survey the entire room.

"That's better," Gary said in a froggy voice. He looked over his shoulder and out the window towards the trees. "Yeah. Okay. This is nice. Maybe I can relax a little here."

I stretched and said, "Well, I'm going to. I hope you can do the same."

He looked at me with big eyes. "You are? You ain't afraid. You're not gonna scribble notes or nothin'?"

"No," I said, looking gently at his wild eyes. "This meeting is just for us to get to know each other."

"Huh! That don't sound like any shrink I've ever met."

"Good!" I chuckled.

He looked at me and chuckled, too. "Okay, Doc. I gotta get serious. I'm in bad trouble. I need help."

Gary had been rated as fifty percent psychiatrically disabled by the Veterans Administration. He worked part time for the post office, where he experienced harassment, especially from his boss, who called him "the .38 killer." He was having a hard time concentrating or restraining his rage and was afraid of losing his job. Gary explained

[5] For such a narrative of one Marine's experience of soul loss in Vietnam during the burning of a Vietnamese village, see Tick, "Vietnam and the American Shadow," 76-77.

some of his difficulties. "I have double vision," he said. Though he saw what was before him at the present moment, he experienced war events as happening simultaneously. "I'll be standing at the post office window selling stamps to an old lady," he said, "and at the same time, I'll be seeing NVA [North Vietnamese Army regulars] charging up the hill at my machine gun post. It takes all the control I can muster to stay right there at my window and just count out change." Gary trusted no one, was numb to all feelings but "staying on red alert." He had to stay distant from everyone for fear he would let his guard down. He often startled, could not sleep or, when he did, had nightmares of combat. "I'm loaded to the gills with survivor's guilt," he said. "I shouldn't be here. I should be dead a thousand times. I'm tellin' you, the things I been through. That's why I'm just waitin' for it. Death is chasing me. It'll catch up to me. It's got to. Nobody could survive what I did and still be alive. Sometimes I'm convinced I'm not."

Gary has obviously heard doctors or other therapists and veterans talk about "survivor's guilt." But when introduced to a new idea, Gary's responses changed. "I can tell you've been scared out of your wits," I said. "You're trembling down to your bones. You had to be through the most horrible things a person can endure. You had to be frightened down to your very soul."

"My soul?" Gary asked. His brow furrowed. "Docs don't talk about souls." His face turned white. He stared at me with pinpoint eyes. "My soul has fled."

"What do you mean?"

"It's gone. It fled my body. I felt it leave."

"Yes. Souls are alive. Souls can enter and souls can leave. Tell me how that happened."

He looked deeply into my eyes, then asked, "You believe me?"

"Yes," I nodded.

He leaned forward, looked deeper. "I believe you do. All right. I'll tell you. It happened at Khe Sanh."

"You were there?"

"The whole damn time! From the end of '67 till we pulled out in June of '68. You know how thick snowflakes fall in the middle of a blizzard?"

"Sure," I said.

"That's how we pounded the hell out of the enemy," Gary said.

"Day and night. Night and day. Air strikes. Heavy bombers. Fighter jets. Heavy and light artillery. My God, I can still feel the earth shaking. In just nine weeks, we dropped 75,000 tons of bombs. I'm tellin' you, Doc, a cockroach couldn't live through what we dropped on them." Gary leaned forward again, staring through me. "But each day, they were charging up my hill again by the thousands. I was a machine gunner. I'd shoot and scream, 'You crazy bastards, don't make me kill you. Stop it! Go home!' They'd fall like flies, but they'd keep comin'. They must have lost ten thousand at Khe Sanh. But they wouldn't stop. It worked too! We were stupid! Khe Sanh was worthless. It was just a blasted pile of mud that nobody wanted. But Westmoreland wasn't gonna lose. Oh God, what we'll do to win! He brought everything we had to Khe Sanh while the gooks spread out in the South and infiltrated everywhere. He fell right into their trap!"

"That's enough to scare the soul out of anybody," I said, looking at him softly.

"Yeah. My soul," Gary said. "Let me tell you what it's like. You can feel the connection between your body and your soul when it starts to break. It's like a thread. You can feel it fraying. I tried so hard, during those long nights with the earth shuddering beneath me, with my hands over my ears. I concentrated so hard to keep that thread from snapping. But it was getting thinner and thinner.

"One day, I had my breakfast in the mess. I sat in the same blue plastic chair in the corner all the time. I felt safer there. Then I went to my post. I was at my machine gun. The same damn thing happened as happened every day. The gooks were comin' up the hill. They were thick that day. They wouldn't stop. They fell by the dozens, but they just climbed over the bodies and kept comin'. God, I could see their eyes.

"Then mortars started fallin' on us. They must have set 'em up to support this charge. This time they were gonna get in. We had to hold the perimeter. I was shootin' and screamin'. I called for more ammo belts. I looked around. I was the only one left. My buddies had split. I looked behind me, and I could see them running like hell toward the base. 'C'mon Gary!' my sarge yelled. In front, the gooks were almost up the hill.

"God, I flew out of that foxhole like lightening. My feet were pounding the mud. I could feel the gooks behind me. I could hear their breathing. Bullets were whizzing by me. I was a goner for sure. That's when it happened."

I didn't take my eyes from his. "Your soul?" I asked.

"I felt it, Doc. The cord snapped. My soul ran right out of my body. It ran faster than me, yards ahead of me. I was exhausted. I wanted to lay down and let them kill me. But it was like I was being pulled along in a jet stream. I couldn't stop. I guess my soul didn't want me to die yet. It saved me."

"That sounds like the only good part."

"No. Wait. I got through our second line. My squad, what was left of it, gathered where it was safe. But I couldn't stop. My soul kept pulling me. I kept running. I ran all the way to the mess. I ran in, like it was safe there, like my blue chair could protect me. Then I stopped dead. I looked. My soul stood next to me and looked. There was a huge hole in the roof over that section of the mess. My blue chair was blown to Kingdom Come. If I would have stayed any longer at breakfast, I'd be in the other world. That was it."

"What?"

"It. The End. I saw my soul shake its head. There was no way it was gonna move back inside my body."

We both breathed deeply and sat a while in silence. "Is it still out?" I asked.

"Yeah," Gary said. "I don't tell anybody this, but it's right here next to me. It's sittin' here looking at you deciding if it's gonna trust you. It's like my twin. It's like there's two of me wherever I go. I can see it and feel it. I got to listen to what it says, y'know. You can't go against your soul."

Gary stared out the window. "It's nice here. I can't believe I told you this. I don't tell nobody. So you tell me, Doc. Is there any way to get your soul back into your body?"

"There is such a thing as soul work," I said. "Native Americans and ancient people knew just what you are talking about. Terror can make the soul flee the body. It's too dangerous to stay in there, so the soul leaves. But then if you don't die, the soul gets stuck. It can't go to the spirit world, because its body is still alive. But it's too scared to climb back into its body."

"Exactly," Gary said. "I was afraid you'd say I'm crazy."

Gary's case is the extreme of dissociation. It is more than the psychic numbing, more than separation of mind from body. It is a removal of the center of experience from the living body without completely snapping the living cord between them. In the presence of extreme life-threatening violence, the soul flees. The center of experience shifts so that the body takes the impact of the trauma but does not feel or register it as deeply without soul presence. With body and soul separated, we are neither living nor dead, but trapped in a limbo in which past and present intermingle without differentiation or continuity. Nothing can feel right unless body and soul rejoin. In ancient times and traditional societies, such soul work was the domain of shamans. Soul loss was a recognized condition, and there were many forms of soul retrieval. Today this work falls to therapists who, too often, are poorly equipped to do it.

"I believe you, Gary," I said. "It's not a crazy thing you're telling me. It's sane," I said. "Your soul splitting from your body at that moment was sane." At this Gary allowed a tight-lipped smile. "We can try to make your body a safe place for your soul to move back to," I said. "If we can get you off combat alert, if you can learn to trust just a little bit, if we can find ways of talking not just to you," I bowed in a gesture of welcome and respect to the air next to Gary, "but to your soul over there, maybe we can bring you two closer together."

Gary nodded, leaned back for the first time, and let his head fall back. He took a deep breath, then sighed. "I've never told anybody this much before," he said. "My soul always stops me at the first sign of disbelief. But now it's out." He looked out the window again. "Yeah," he sighed. "It's not bad here. Maybe I can learn to relax a little."

Soul Loss as Response to Violence

A middle-aged woman was hunting with friends, a few of whom were novices at the sport. She returned to their van to warm herself. A friend stood by her window and saw a deer break loose through the woods on the far side of the road. Without thinking or aiming, the friend raised his rifle and shot through the van windows. The bullet blasted past the woman's head and ricocheted around the inside of the van, just missing her several times before it wedged in the seat by her side. In many ways this woman had a similar experience to Gary's. She felt her soul flee her body in terror at that moment, and she also reported a double life. Her soul, she said, was attached by a thin, living cord. During therapy sessions, she pointed to it, floating in the air over her shoulder. She would turn to it and listen to what it said to her, then report her soul's comments to me. What appeared crazy to her family felt sane and inevitable to her.

Body-soul splitting is only one way that a soul exposed to severe threat manifests its lost condition. One man, a consultant, arranged his office like an interrogation chamber. He had a long, narrow room that was empty and unlighted for most of its length. Clients and consultant had to walk down the dark, barren corridor to the far end where his chair was set up in front of a narrow couch, with a single spot light shining on the couch where his clients sat. He was Jewish and had been a child during the Nazi occupation of his country. His parents were deported to concentration camps, but he escaped and was hidden for several years by friends, neighbors, and strangers. "My formative experience," he said, "was not surviving. It was fleeing from one dangerous haven to the next. I felt as if all the powers of the universe pointed their destructive weapons only at me."

This man's soul dwelt in a perpetual darkness. It could only function in a setting that simultaneously replicated a refuge in the underground and an interrogation chamber in which the destructive forces might have seated him. His soul lived and worked in hiding from a world that sought his destruction. He was in the hot-seat, being both interrogated for destruction and tortured for surviving.

Another woman client had been left behind in Warsaw when her parents, active members of the resistance, fled the Nazis. She had been deported for extermination and only saved while on a cattle car by the timely arrival of Allied troops. Then, at age six, during the Communist occupation of Poland, she had had to flee across country with her two younger sisters. All her adult life she experienced an impossibility of love and safety. No amount of pleading for pity or reassurance from lovers or husbands, no degree of professional success, no amount of obsessive control or planning could provide this woman's soul with the deepening, centering, or belonging she craved. Instead she lived for decades in a puddle of tears and terror. It was as if, with the dawn of each day, with the attempt to connect and root in every therapy session, she had to begin anew in the cattle cars and discover whether she would live or die.

The primary movement in all these souls is toward a survival in which they can hardly believe. Their deepening is into the darkness as if they had roots that stretched far into the Underworld but sent no sprouts into the light. The destructive and degenerative aspects of life penetrated their souls so that they could not believe in or experience the counterbalancing, regenerative powers. As a result it was only with the greatest effort that they were able to eat, sleep, work, or maintain relationships.

Extreme violence demolishes the normally rigid barrier between the day world and the dark, inner world. These worlds now interpenetrate. Time as continuity, as past and present, disappears. It is replaced by a simultaneity of actual and remembered events and an eternal presence of horror. Finally, all the choices for these lost souls between what is good or bad for them are reduced to questions of safety and survival. It is good to be alive for one more day. It is good to eat this meal. It is good to feel safe for this hour. It is good not to hurt another or to be hurt by another at this moment. Those principles that were experienced as ultimate in the fields of danger become their ethical codes. These souls are lost because they are trapped in disconnection. They can neither leave the ecology of horror nor balance it with principles and experiences from the day world.

Dead Souls

Americans still have over 2,000 missing in action from the Vietnam War, and the Vietnamese record over 250,000 missing in action. The war was so brutal with its massive bombings, napalm, white phosphorous, Agent Orange, and other destructive modern weaponry that such numbers are not surprising. In Vietnamese Buddhist belief, after death a soul cannot move on from this world to the spirit world if the person is not given proper burial rites. Today many Vietnamese people report that theirs is a country of lost souls trapped in the limbo between the physical and spiritual planes, unable to continue their karmic journeys. Vietnamese and American teams have made great efforts to recover as many of their missing as possible.

> If you can't identify them by name, we'll be burdened by their deaths for the rest of our lives," the head of the MIA

> team had said... His entire life was gathering corpses. He was preoccupied with this sole duty... He used to describe his work as though it were a sacred oath, and ask others to swear their dedication."[6]

While the search continues, Vietnamese people report encounters with these unreleased souls:

> ...His group had found a half-buried coffin. It had popped up like a termite hill on a riverbank... Inside the coffin was a thick plastic bag, similar to the ones Americans used for their dead, but this one was clear plastic. The soldier seemed to be still breathing, as though in deep sleep... His handsome, youthful face had a serious air, and his body appeared to be still warm... Then before their eyes the plastic bag discoloured, whitening as though suddenly filled with smoke. The bag glowed and something seemed to escape from it, causing the bag to deflate. When the smoke cleared, only a yellowish ash remained. Kien and his platoon were astounded and fell to their knees around it, raising their hands to heaven praying for a safe flight for the departed soul...[7]

They also report hearing or seeing these lost souls crying in anguish, begging for help to be released from limbo and move on:

> Sometimes the dead manifested themselves as sounds rather than shadows. Others in the MIA team...said they'd heard the dead playing musical instruments and singing. They said...deep inside the ancient forest, the ageless trees whispered along with a song that merged into harmony with an ethereal guitar, singing, *O victorious years and months, O endless suffering and pain.*[8]

An even more grievous sense of souls lost to violence is found in Zulu and some other traditional people's beliefs. One of the most gruesome forms of killing perpetrated against blacks in South Africa during apartheid was called "necklacing." In necklacing "the person's head is tied into a tire filled with gasoline, and he is burned alive..." Stephen Larsen, the editor of *Song of the Stars* by Vusamazulu Credo

[6] Bao Ninh, *The Sorrow of War* (London: Minerva, 1994), 84.

[7] *Ibid.*, 83

[8] *Ibid.*, 82.

Mutwa, comments on the cruel effects of this practice: "'Necklacing' is horrible to the African traditionalist, because it is believed that if a person dies in this manner, his or her very soul, as well as the body, perishes."[9] These souls, the Zulus believe, are not lost and wandering but destroyed and lost forever. Other forms of killing throughout history had similar aims. The medieval practice of burning at the stake was not done solely to purify the offending soul of sin. Rather some beliefs held that death by fire destroyed the soul. Therefore, burning at the stake can be imagined as an attempt not merely to kill enemies and terrify their survivors into submission but to eradicate the souls of offenders or enemies from the cosmos.[10] Given the folk beliefs of a people against whom a society wages war, particular forms of destruction may not be aimed at the people, military, culture, or political systems we call enemies but against their souls.

The pragmatic perspective argues that there would naturally be a significant number of people missing in action from such a brutal war as the one waged in Vietnam. Is it possible that our long-standing national anguish over this issue unites us with our former enemies? Is it possible that we Americans sense in some soulful place that the souls of the missing and the violently slain are not at peace, and that they cannot be at peace until we recover their bodies and their names and propitiate their souls? Perhaps unknowingly our anguish corresponds with ancient folk and religious beliefs that rituals, sacrifices, and offerings on the part of the living are necessary to aid the souls of the dead.

Awareness of the lost souls of the dead brings us to an archetypal understanding of some recurring nightmares suffered by war survivors. Such nightmares are one of the most common and troublesome symptoms of Post-traumatic Stress Disorder. In their sleep, former soldiers see their comrades or their enemies killed over and over again. Or they see the dead return to them, sometimes looking alive, sometimes as living dead. If the souls of the killed are lost and wandering, perhaps it is not just a traumatic memory impression that plagues the survivor. James Hillman's argument that dreams are paths to the Underworld through which the images of the invisible can

---

[9] Vusamazulu Credo Mutwa, *Song of the Stars*, Ed. Stephen Larsen (Barrytown, New York: Station Hill, 1996), xxviii.

[10] Stephen Larsen, personal communication.

return to us as visible is helpful here. With Post-traumatic Stress Disorder, nightmares of the dead may serve as gateways to the Underworld through which the restless lost souls can return to the living and cry to them for aid. Perhaps in their dreamlife, war survivors perceive, as Odysseus did on his descent to Hades, shades of the dead gathering and pressing on them with their anguish.

Like our veterans, Odysseus was a survivor of a brutal war. He became lost on the homeward journey and could not complete it without first successfully descending to the Underworld and meeting, in addition to Tireseas and his mother, the restless souls of dead comrades. In fact the first command Odysseus received in the Underworld was from his unburied soldier, Elpenor, who was "missing in action" on Circe's isle. Elpenor's shade instructed Odysseus to return to his death site and give his body proper burial. The witnesses of Homer, the Vietnamese people, and veterans' nightmares are all saying that warriors cannot complete their return without putting their missing in action comrades' souls to rest. In classical belief, the dead needed an offering of live blood in order to speak. Odysseus slew a black ewe and ram to provide that blood. In our era it may be the living blood of survivors that the souls of the dead, during dreamtime, gather to drink.

Recovering Souls Lost in War

What possibilities exist for aiding these souls lost in the war zones of the world? It is their very lost condition that can lead us to clues for their, and our, recovery. If we let ourselves hear their anguish, theirs seems to be the sanest response to past, horrific conditions. Ironically those most difficult to help are not those suffering from this disorder. Rather, the most frightening survivors are those who, after a sojourn in Hell, still display a strong ego—those who are not disturbed, do not feel pain and loss, do not worry for their souls.

One woman in psychotherapy, the daughter of a traumatized World War II veteran, learned firsthand how frightening such people can be. Just out of high school, she married a young Vietnam combat veteran. They divorced, and she lived with a Polish survivor of Nazi labor camps for twenty years. He drank himself into a stupor every night during which he beat and sexually abused her. "I thought his soul was strong and beautiful because he didn't show any pain or disturbance," she said. A strong ego displayed in response to horrible experiences is a form of denial and soul loss. "I thought my own soul was weak and petty because I hurt so badly, and my pain made it difficult for me to function. Through therapy I realized that my pain, fear, and sorrow was a sign that my soul was still alive and kicking, while the souls of all my men were lost, damaged, or dead." Those people whose souls are lost due to their time in war are the ones who have the most to teach us about the effects of violence on soul. But how can we make soul out of this lost condition?

Recovering the Memory of Soul Loss

The souls of those lost in war can be imagined as still wandering in the war zone. The psyche has been so impacted by horror that horror has replaced present reality as the landscape of soul. It is critical that such people develop this awareness that they are lost and stuck in the horror. They must rediscover how, when, and where their soul loss occurred. Psychotherapy and other forms of healing can then become the imaginal quest for lost souls.

Commonly, war survivors suffering Post-Traumatic Stress Disorder are trapped in the ecology of war, using all their defenses, including a strong ego, to avoid feeling the pain and terror of their condition. It typically takes recognition of the soul loss and familiarity with the ecology of war for the guide to steadily lead the survivor to the recognition of soul loss. The survivor must be willing to descend to the Underworld and wander the landscape of horror yet again. But this time a second descent into the war zone can be done imaginally. Memories and their accompanying feelings can and should be relived not solely as traumatic events needing catharsis and witness but as a means to soul restoration. Despite a human reluctance to once again visit the fields of horror, the imaginal descent becomes a personal odyssey into the Underworld in search for one's lost soul.

During war, soldiers are transformed from complex human beings into instruments of destruction. Even if at war for highly moral purposes—such as ending genocide or preserving the lives of loved ones—men and women become servants of Ares, the savage god, the destroyer. To effect this transformation, soldiers undergo a moral inversion wherein good and evil, creation and destruction, life and death, exchange places in the soul. The souls of warriors realign with the values, forces, and syntax of death and destruction. According to Socrates, the soul is that which distinguishes the good, and the good life consists in choosing what is good for the soul. Thus, in order to return from the inner landscape of war, a soul must realign its ethical system, leaving off its loyalty to the god of destruction and recovering what is life-affirming and good for soul.

Reconciliation with the Dead

Traditional peoples tell us that the living are responsible for the souls of the dead. Some Native Americans teach that this responsibility extends even to our enemies. "When you kill an enemy warrior, you become responsible for his soul."[11] If warriors do not propitiate the souls of their dead, including their enemies, that soul is trapped and can turn against and harm the survivor. But if properly propitiated, its powers can enter the survivor. Without proper attendance to the souls of the dead, then souls of both dead and living are lost.

There are many ways to support war survivors in their attempts to reconcile with the dead. Through active imagination techniques in psychotherapy, one man who was a medic in Vietnam spent most of two years slowly revisiting all the dead and wounded he had worked with in his firebase emergency room. Each of the victims had moved into his soul space and haunted him. We staged encounters with these suffering souls one by one, sought to discover what they still wanted from him, talked to them, and released them, thereby freeing the soul of this former medic to live his life.

Veterans often seek reconciliation with the dead. The popularity of the Vietnam Memorial Wall in Washington, the thousands of letters, photographs, and mementos left there, attests to the desire for this reconciliation. It also underlies the need for ritual. Journeys can be planned and guided to important sites such as the Vietnam Memorial, battlefields, countries abroad in which people fought, and cemeteries in order to commune with the spirits of the dead. Service to the living in those places, such as some Vietnam veterans have done in Vietnam, aid the reconciliation process.

Rituals can be staged in and out of the therapy setting to promote reconciliation with the dead. A veterans combat group I lead held a memorial fire on a mountain top one Memorial Day night. It was

[11] General Grant, Lakota Elder, personal communication.

staged in the watchfire tradition, in which fires in home villages would be kept burning until all wandering warriors out on the warpath had returned safely home. This group burned a memorial watchfire to guide the souls of their dead comrades home to the spirit world. They prayed, told stories, cried out their comrades' names to the stars, thanked them, and vowed to release them. During imaginal conversations with the dead, war survivors often receive messages such as "choose life," "live for me," "return to the land of the living," and "I'm glad you made it home."

Many war survivors wish to be as they were before their military experience. They cry out to have their young, innocent selves and all their lost years returned to them. These cries are of souls in anguish at what they have seen, felt, and learned. They are cries from the Underworld by souls that have not yet returned.

War is an extreme form of descent into the Underworld. At first it may feel like a forced, unwilling descent. But during war survivors learn what they never wanted to know about individual, human, and earthly nature. It was to attain this wisdom that the descent was made. To return from war, survivors must develop new identities as witnesses to the Underworld. They must grow these identities large enough so that they surround and carry the traumatic experiences. Thye must call soul back into service as the community's witness to both the shadow and the aesthetic of war. Warriors, then, know the love of war. This is not to love destruction or killing.

Souls are likely to have become wounded or lost during war through their exposure to horror and violence. The way for souls to return to life is by way of consent. "I had this experience. I needed it. I have taken the difficult road. I have been initiated. I am now a warrior and will serve the code and embody the quality of warriors—courage, nobility, duty, honor, loyalty, steadfastness of principle, comradely love all my days." It is by becoming a warrior again that soul lost in war may return.

The Numinous Horse: This So Greatly Loved Body

DEBRA S. KNOWLES

Far back, far back in our dark soul the horse prances.
D. H. Lawrence (Apocalypse)

No fear shatters me when wild horses take me as far as they can.
Nietzsche (Ronell 129)

Crime and Punishment contains what must surely be one of the most chilling passages in literature: Rodion Raskolnikov's dream of himself as a child witnessing a cart horse being hideously beaten to death by drunken peasants. Coming too close, the boy Rodion is whipped by one of the men striking the horse. Later, after he commits his murder, Raskolnikov is again whipped by a coachman, symbolically merging man and horse (Friedman, 168). Dostoevsky would return to the image of a horse, one whipped about the eyes, in *The Brothers Karamazov.*[1]

[1] Citation refers to excerpted chapters from *The Brothers Karamazov* published as *The Grand Inquisitor.*

Debra Smith Knowles is a graduate of Stanford University and Pacifica Graduate Institute. This essay is an excerpt from her doctoral dissertation in Mythological Studies at Pacifica.

In 1878, Friedrich Theodor Vischer, a well-known German philosopher (whose philosophy Nietzsche scathingly attacked in his autobiography, *Ecce Homo*) published an autobiographical novel titled *Auch Einer* (*Another One*), containing the following scene: A. E., the protagonist, encounters a carter maltreating his tired horse. He interferes and tries to stop him; a wild scuffle ensues in the course of which A. E. grabs the carter's whip and starts flogging him, whereupon the latter draws his butcher's knife and fatally stabs his assailant (Grimm, 204).

The spring before the winter of his insanity, Friedrich Nietzsche wrote a letter to a friend celebrating an uncharacteristic bout of good health (his first good spring in fifteen years), and the news that lectures on his philosophy were being given at the University of Copenhagen.[2] In an otherwise cheerful report, Nietzsche inserted the following:

> Yesterday I imagined a scene Diderot would have described as "maudlin morality." Winter landscape. An old carter, with an expression of the most brutal cynicism, harder even than the surrounding winter, is relieving himself against the side of his horse. The horse, poor abused creature, looks back gratefully, very gratefully... (Fuss, 118).

In early January 1889, while walking the streets of Turin, Nietzsche came upon a coachman beating a horse...and apparently stepped into Raskolnikov's dream (Friedman, 170). Tearfully, he embraced the horse and collapsed. His sanity left him although his body lived another eleven years.

> *Your soul will be dead even before your body: therefore fear nothing any more!*
> (Nietzsche, *Zarathustra,* 48)

What is it about a horse, a mistreated horse, that so caught the imagination of these late nineteenth century figures who brought to our attention that God had disappeared and no longer spoke to His people? These men, so impressed with the image of an abused horse, grappled all their lives with the riddle of suffering. The response of Nietzsche was to embrace suffering as fate ("what does not kill me makes me stronger"), a philosophy distilled into the "eternal recurrence

[2] Letter to Reinhard von Seydlitz, 13 May 1888.

of the same" and *amor fati*; of Vischer, to ascend to a place of cosmic irony and humor; and Dostoevsky, while appearing to remain within the Christian ethos, nevertheless gave the best lines to those who could not accept a world in which such suffering could exist (190).[3]

> *...a feeble little nag has foundered under too heavy a load and cannot move. The peasant beats it, beats it savagely...thrashes it mercilessly over and over again...But that's only a horse, and God has given horses to be beaten.*
> (Dostoevsky, *The Grand Inquisitor*, 11)

Although they never met (Nietzsche discovered Dostoevsky in 1887), Nietzsche and Dostoevsky can be seen to be on parallel courses, inspired by the same archetypal themes and symbols. Nietzsche wrote of the effect the Russian author had on him: "Dostoevsky happened to me as Stendhal did earlier, by sheer accident...and the sudden awareness that one has met with a brother" and "he has given me my most precious psychological material" (Friedman, 153). The similarities in their thinking included the ideas of the death of God, "all is permitted," "nothing happens by chance," man becoming a god, the importance of dreams, and horses.

> *As soon as men have all of them denied God...*
> *the man-god will appear...Let us...become gods."*
> (Dostoevsky, *The Brothers Karamazov*, xii, 788*ff*)

> *God is dead!...I teach you the Superman.*
> (Nietzsche, *Zarathustra*, 41)

Fate marked Nietzsche for his encounter with the horse. He was born on October 15, the date of the ancient Roman horse sacrifice. The sight of the beaten horse triggered something in Nietzsche, something that to sane eyes looked like a fall from the tightrope he walked during his life.[4] If, as C. G. Jung said, animals are the shadows of the gods (*MDR*, 216), then what god appeared to Nietzsche? What message did this presence wish to convey through his prophet? What words did Nietzsche whisper to the horse? Milan Kundera imagines that

---

[3] Cf. Ivan Karamazov's dialogue with Alyosha, Book V, Chapters 3, 4 and 5.

[4] Nietzsche had made the claim that voluntarily going mad was the only sane thing to do, leading to speculation that his insanity was faked.

Nietzsche apologized to the horse for Descartes who denied animals their souls (288); David Miller reminds us that the horse had a closer experience of Nietzsche's collapse than we may ever achieve (161). And why would this presence become manifest in dream and imagination (and, to Nietzsche, finally, in flesh) to the men most responsible for promulgating the credo that "God is dead"?—we are tempted to say, a presence that before it destroyed Nietzsche first drove him mad.

> *Hast thou given the horse strength? Hast thou clothed his neck with thunder?*
> ("The Book of Job" 39:19)

> *People of a more enlightened future may examine [spurs and crops and bits as fierce as weapons] and shake their heads in wonder and dismay. Whatever possessed our ancestors, those people may ask, to use such barbaric instruments on an animal so noble, so sweetly disposed, as the horse?*
> (Scanlan, 258*)*

It can be imagined from a certain perspective that psychologically, the properties of the horse belong to the unconscious of humanity: clairvoyant, clairaudient, pathfinding, with mantic powers (Jung, *CW 5*, § 421); the horse helps us find our way when we are lost. In Vedic India, Hindu dying gods often assumed horse shape, and Hindu queens performed rituals involving the insertion of a sacrificed horse's penis between their legs. The blood-wedding of the Earth Mother and the Horse's Penis produced the race of horse-gods known in the Aegean as Centaurs, in India as Asvins or Gandharvas. They were great wizards, skilled musicians and dancers, expert healers and "lusty lovers of women" (Walker, 412). In Nordic mythology the horse is also a symbol of the dying and resurrecting god Odin/Wotan, who hung nine days on Yggdrasil—drasil means both "gallows tree" and "horse," and Yggr is Odin's title as Lord of Death. One of Odin's epithets is *Völsi*, translatable both as "Son of God" and "Horse's Penis." Jung writes that it was Nietzsche's classical training and unfamiliarity with Germanic mythology that caused him to name his god Dionysos, but that, in actuality, it was Wotan who inspirited and possessed him (*CW 10*, § 373-394), and that there are ancient connections between Wotan and the figures of Christ and

Dionysus (373). Thus, an integral element of the mystery of dying and resurrecting gods had been sexuality—until Christ.

To be in the presence of a horse is to be aware of body. One can feel its physicality, libido, and energy. Not surprisingly a common response to the horse is awe and fear of this creature that is more powerful than we but who serves us.[5] By nature the horse is the animal of flight, but it has overcome this instinct to the extent that our histories and legends are full of tales of the horse's courage and nobility.

> *Why has the self created the body? ...we might be forms made of air and beyond sex or appetites or digestion and such nuisances, but it is a fact that we have bodies which have been created by the self, so we must assume that the self really means us to live in the body, to live that experiment, live our lives... So you must inquire what experiment the self wants to make.*
>
> (Jung, *Nietzsche,* 120)

What is this body that the horse so exquisitely symbolizes? In his five-year lecture series on Nietzsche's *Zarathustra,* Jung spoke of the connection between the body and consciousness:

> It is the essential metaphysical meaning of the earth that it gives specification to things, that it makes things distinct... And really the essence of differentiation, the idea of the self, could not exist for one single moment if there were not a body to create and maintain that distinctness (45)... The body is the truest thing; this is indubitable and undeniable even if it should fabricate poetry and philosophy (92).

For Jung, the body is the "guarantee of consciousness," the instrument by which meaning is created; therefore, "there can be no meaning without the body" (94). Nietzsche was aware of this. In *Zarathustra* (whose name derives from the Persian word for horse or camel), he reviles those who would escape the misery of the body by inventing

[5] In a recent book, author Monty Roberts relates his experiences trying to alter the relationship of human beings and horses. "For centuries humans have said to horses you do what I tell you or I'll hurt you... At heart I am saying that no one has the right to say you must to an animal—or to another human." (244-245). His occasional public demonstrations working with abused horses often stirs buried emotions in onlookers. "For many in the audience who have themselves been abused, the horse in the ring becomes an almost too-potent metaphor." (245)

Heaven: "Now they thought themselves transported from their bodies and from this earth, these ingrates. Yet to what do they owe the convulsion and joy of their transport? To their bodies and to this earth"(60). The Self wants us to live in the body, and the horse is the "symbol par excellence for the libido that is leading us—through sacrifice—to the mandala, to the Self" (Hannah).

There is more reason in your body than in your best wisdom.
(Zarathustra, 61-62*)*

We live in a time that is heir to the sense that God has disappeared. People may accept or reject this notion, but after Nietzsche one cannot easily ignore it (Friedman, 141-3). Just as Nietzsche called Socrates a "pesty horsefly, set by a god on the neck of the beautiful horse Athens," so David Miller calls Nietzsche "our Socrates, our gadfly, stung by the horse he himself stung!" (169). It would appear that this age calls for us to find the immanent god, to ourselves become gods. For Nietzsche "closeness to the divine is not tolerable" and a god's presence keeps humans from becoming all that they can be (Friedman, 187). Yet, while we might believe that we have outgrown God, defeated our need for Him, it may well be that the "deity acquiesces in the human appropriation of powers from the divine realm" (191).

Nietzsche apparently did not consider that the death he felt was not of God but of a moribund god-image. It is not hard to imagine that the sight of a powerful, mute, essentially innocent animal at the mercy of weaker, more brutish creatures would evoke great pity from a soul as sensitive as his. If we have no one to blame but ourselves, then only the coachman can stop the coachman's hand; in Dostoevsky's words we become "responsible to all for all" (*Karamazov*, Book VI). "If God is dead, then each of us is responsible for our dreams and any good or evil in the world would be our own doing" (Jung, *Nietzsche*, 34). A beaten horse becomes a symbol of human and divine suffering and points to the paradox of good and evil and their apparent inseparability.

Nietzsche was no nihilist; he wanted to move us beyond a sterile and fragmented Christianity. Two thousand years of suppressing and projecting evil had failed, and Nietzsche was looking for a philosophy that would lead us out of peril and beyond despair. In that sense, he was the precursor to Jung and to depth psychology's different approach to evil: to imagine that we exist, in part, to make God aware of a dark side that includes evil, the body, femininity, and sexuality.

The horse connects us to sexuality, to the body, to Odin/Wotan, Dionysos and Christ. The horse in harness, scourged by humans, mirrors the image of a tortured Christ carrying the Cross. But the horse also symbolizes what has been left out of Christianity[6]—the dark soul where, D. H. Lawrence writes, "the horse prances" (101). If God sought to experience mortal, finite, bodily existence, why would we insist that He never experienced the supreme physical act, the sexual one? And that He had never known the love of a woman? Sacred sexuality, after centuries lying buried in esoterica and hidden in the image of Mary Magdalene, may be finding its way into the myth. The words in the title of this paper—"this so greatly loved body"—are Rilke's, from his essay on Rodin's sculpture of Mary Magdalene embracing Jesus on the cross, her naked form wrapped around his (Haskins, 355). The Magdalene represents the human side of the divine-human equation, with whom Jesus might have experienced bodily love.

With what emotions does the archetype symbolized by the horse announce its presence? To the dreaming Raskolnikov the sight of the whipped and beaten horse brings tears to his eyes, "his heart swells up," he sobs and cannot catch his breath, "screaming, he forces a path for himself through the crowd…" He takes up the bloody head of the dead horse and "kisses it, kisses it on the eyes, on the lips…" (Friedman, 166-168). Nor could Nietzsche resist the creature before him. He, too, broke into tears. He, too, embraced the horse.

---

[6] The linking of body, sex, and the feminine is not ontological but rather circumstantial (of course sexuality can be carried by both the masculine and the feminine). Yet sex, body, and females have been often relegated to the unconscious.

Works Cited

Dostoevsky, Feodor. *Crime and Punishment.* Ed. George Gibian. 3rd Edition. New York and London: W. W. Norton, 1989.

______. *The Grand Inquisitor.* Ed. Charles B. Guignon. Trans. Constance Garnett. Indianapolis and Cambridge: Hackett Publishing, 1993.

Friedman, Richard Elliott. *The Disappearance of God: A Divine Mystery.* Boston: Little, Brown, 1995.

Fuss, Peter and Henry Shapiro, eds. *Nietzsche: A Self-Portrait from His Letters.* Cambridge: Harvard UP, 1971.

Grimm, Reinhold. "Embracing Two Horses: Tragedy, Humor, and Inwardness; or, Nietzsche, Visher, and Julius Bahnsen." *Neitzsche-Studien.* Vol. 18. Berlin: Walter de Gruyter, 1989, 203-220.

Hannah, Barbara. "The Symbolism of Animals." Twelve Lectures Given at the C. G. Jung Institute, Zürich. October 28, 1957-February 17, 1958.

Haskins, Susan. *Mary Magdalen: Myth and Metaphor.* New York: Riverhead Books, 1993.

Jung, C. G. *Collected Works.* Princeton: Princeton UP, 1980.

______. *Memories, Dreams, Reflections.* Ed. Aniela Jaffé. Trans. Richard and Clara Winston. New York: Vintage Books, 1965; rev. ed. 1989.

______. *Seminar on Nietzsche's Zarathustra.* Ed. James L. Jarrett. Abridged Edition. Princeton: Princeton UP, 1998.

Kundera, Milan. *The Unbearable Lightness of Being.* Trans. M. Heim. New York: HarperPerennial, 1984.

Lawrence, D. H. *Apocalypse.* London: Penguin Books, 1995.

Miller, David L. "Nietzsche's Horse and Other Tracings of the Gods." *Stanford Italian Review*, 1986, vol. 6, 159-170.

Nietszche, Friedrich. *Beyond Good and Evil.* Trans. Walter Kaufmann. New York: Random House, 1989.

______. *Thus Spoke Zarathustra.* Trans. R. J. Hollingdale. London: Penguin, 1969.

Roberts, Monty. *The Man who Listens to Horses.* New York: Random House, 1997.

Ronell, Avital. "Hitting the Streets: *Ecce Fama.*" *Stanford Italian Review*, Vol. 6, 1986, 119-140.

Scanlan, Lawrence. "Afterword." *The Man Who Listens to Horses.* New York: Random House, 1997. 239-58.

Walker, Barbara. *The Woman's Encyclopedia of Myths and Secrets.* San Francisco: HarperCollins, 1983.

Mickey Mantle Meets Prometheus

MIKE DENNEY

On June 8, 1995, Mickey Mantle had a liver transplant. His cirrhotic, diseased liver was surgically removed and replaced with a healthy one from an organ donor. "The Mick" had been given a new organ of metabolism, an organ which the ancient Greeks called the "seat of the soul." This country boy who had risen to fame, this Titan of baseball whose phenomenal statistics included 536 home runs and a .299 lifetime batting average, was resting in the intensive care unit after undergoing successful surgery, as the news media told his worshipful public.

Although liver transplantation was no longer rare—it was being performed regularly without fanfare in medical centers across the country—Mickey's celebrity status demanded that the reporters cover the story. They said he had been the beneficiary of one of the great scientific advances of modern medicine, a procedure developed over the past forty years by Doctor Starzl, a giant of the surgical world. The reporters extolled Mickey's surgical team, which consisted of internists, immunologists, surgeons, social workers, and special nurses, all working together to make the operation a success. Like Mickey,

Mike Denney has practiced medicine and surgery for forty years. He is the author of *Second Opinion* (Grosset & Dunlap, 1979) and is currently a doctoral student in depth psychology at Pacifica Graduate Institute.

the doctors also had heroic statistics—overall survival rates of eighty percent for one year, seventy-three percent for three years and sixty-nine percent for five years (UNOS, 1998).

One might imagine that if the news of this scientific and technological triumph of humanity over disease reached the home of the Greek gods on Mount Olympus, Prometheus, the mythological benefactor of humanity and the father of the arts and sciences, might have been pleased. It was this Titan who favored mortals over the gods and who stole the power of fire from the heavens and carried it to humans for their use. Surely, Prometheus would be proud of the hubris of both Mickey Mantle and his modern surgeons— Mickey who with one swing of his bat could hit the ball out of the park and into the heavens, and his surgeons who with their science had the ability to enter the human body, remove the seat of the soul, and replace it with donor parts to rescue mortals from the inexorable call of Hades.

Is it possible that Prometheus would have been pleased in a deeper way? Would he not have been beside himself with joy to know that mere human beings had found a way to do something for Mickey Mantle that only the gods had been able to do for Prometheus? If we look at it with a mythic sensibility, might we imagine that Prometheus was the first patient in Western culture to undergo liver transplantation?

According to the myth, Prometheus had been bound to the Caucasus mountain for an eternity of suffering because Zeus had become angered at the Titan's hubris, his thievery, and his failure to offer proper respect and sacrifice to the gods. Held firmly by a mantle of unbreakable chains, Prometheus was tortured by an eagle who pecked out his liver every day. The consumed portions of his liver would grow back each night only to be eaten again the next day. However, reflecting upon Prometheus' plight from the perspectives of modern medical science and Mickey Mantle's surgery, we remember that when the liver attempts to regenerate, it grows mostly scar tissue resulting in cirrhosis, and the new cells that do resemble normal liver tissue are formed in anatomical disarray. For Prometheus, these cells might have provided suitable food for eagles but would have been unable to perform their vital functions. To escape, and ultimately to be granted a place on Olympus, Prometheus needed to be rid of the chains and the offending eagle, but he also needed a liver transplant, a replacement for the seat of his soul. So, with some trickery, he convinced Zeus to help.

Who would be on Prometheus' surgical transplant team? Following the ancient myth, the chief surgeon was, of course, Hercules, the hero who had the ability to heal wounded warriors and power over epidemics but who also had a bad habit of causing unintended chaos, even death. We might imagine that Apollo, the physician, could have been the consultant in internal medicine. Artemis and Aphrodite might have suggested herbs and plants, Athene had the magic of the Gorgon blood for immunosuppression, and Hermes was the social worker.

And, who would be the organ donor? Perhaps Chiron, the kindly centaur who had himself taught Asclepius the art of medicine and was healthy except that he had been struck with an arrow and suffered a life-threatening injury, a wound that would never heal. He was a perfect liver donor. Like the present-day donor for Mickey Mantle, an ordinary citizen with a donor-card driver's license, Chiron offered his own soul to Hades so that Prometheus might continue on. Hercules, the surgeon, dissected away the chains and excised the eagle. Hermes, the psychopomp, escorted Chiron to Hades while Prometheus, with his new seat of soul, having learned the sin of *hubris* and the ritual of sacrifice, was granted a divine state on Mount Olympus where he thereafter performed many services for the gods.

Viewed from the peaks of mountain tops and ivory towers, our stories are of triumph and ascension to the realm of the gods. But soul, and the seat of soul, resides also in the vales (Hillman, 1979, 55-62). Prometheus' liver could probably only heal in the shadow of night (Slater, 1998). So, let us descend into the valley where shadows cast new light and in whose depths melancholia (the black bile of diseased liver), may be washed in refreshing streams which flow to the sea.

Prometheus' myth is one among the gods. Mickey's is a human story. The eagle eating away at his liver was alcohol and was not slain even by a Herculean effort. The chains binding him were addiction and were not easily broken. His operation was unsuccessful. He was found also to have cancer of the lung and kidney disease. After lingering for two months, our baseball hero died of cancer and heart failure on August 13, 1995. The alcohol had damaged his heart as well as the seat of his soul. The doctors with all their science had not understood the extent of his affliction—nor the limitations of their technological skills.

There was a public outcry after Mickey's death. How could the doctors offer a precious donor liver to a sixty-three year-old who had been drinking alcohol heavily up to just a few months before the operation when there were other, younger, more deserving patients? What were the assurances that Mickey would not have continued to drink and thereby destroy his new liver after the operation? Why had not the doctors diagnosed the cancer beforehand and then given the donor liver to someone with a better prognosis? How could the doctors have such god-like hubris to give a celebrity, who had been on the waiting list only forty-eight hours, higher priority than other ordinary and more needy recipients who had been on the list for years? What should be the guiding principles for a medical procedure in which one person must die for another to live, and in which there were currently ten thousand more potential recipients than there were donors? Why should wealthy people get donated livers in preference to those who are poor?

The media exposure about the plight of this national celebrity raised questions about the ethics and soul of medical science. Many people wondered: How could it be that modern medical science posed so many seemingly unanswerable questions about humans beings' relationships to one another and to the gods?

II

Science was not a problem in early shamanic healing. Shamans were the ultimate generalists who practiced "soul retrieval" in an ecstatic connection to the gods and animal totems (Achterberg, 1995). Gradually this form of healing gathered more and more "science" to it as the shamans learned herbal remedies, bone-setting, and perhaps remedies borrowed from animals (Chambom, 1997, 8-11). Many centuries later in ancient Greek temples called Aesclapions, this soulful healing was continued as patients offered sacrifices and approached the healing god Asclepius in dream or meditation (Ellenberger, 1970, 32-34). Asclepius was the Greek god of healing whose caduceus, with its snakes coiled around a staff, remains the symbol of Western medicine.

We might remember that even Asclepius, the mythical son of Apollo, had been warned about hubris in his science. When Asclepius restored a dead man to life, Hades was furious, and Zeus, noting that no one should thwart nature or interfere with the ultimate destiny of mortals, struck Asclepius with a thunderbolt. Like Prometheus and Mickey Mantle's surgeons, Asclepius was warned against excessive pride and arrogance.

In the temple of Aesclepius on the Island of Cos in 400 B.C.E. the science of Western medicine began. There Hippocrates, a human physician, struggled with the fundamental power of science in healing. While offering sacrifices in the temple of healing to the gods and spirits, Hippocrates kept glancing over his shoulder at the patient lying alone, apparently receiving the blessings of health through divine presence. Hippocrates could not resist his curiosity. He turned away from the sacrificial altar and went, instead, to his patient's bedside. There, in a personal relationship, Hippocrates began to talk to his patients, to examine them with his senses, and to record his observations. He noticed such things as facial expression, the palms of the hands, the pulses, the emotional state, the breathing patterns, and many other characteristics. Gradually, he began to relate his findings to the nature and the treatment of diseases. Hippocrates had invented the science of medicine.

In doing so Hippocrates did not forget the sacrificial altar. He took it with him to his patient's bedside and immediately recognized that hubris on the part of the physician could be harmful to the patient. He said, "First do no harm," and then created the basic medical ethics of Western civilization which began with an oath to the gods—saying, "I swear by Apollo the physician, and Asclepius, and all the gods and goddesses..." Hippocrates understood that the power of medical science could lead to hubris and would have to be balanced by respect and honor for the divine and for soul. A few centuries later, Aristotle carried forward the Hippocratic ideals. In addition to his interests in biology, physics, and physiology, which won for him the title of "father of biological sciences," he wrote extensively on soul, which he believed resided not only in humans but in all living things.

However, in the medical field, the hubris of science soon reigned supreme. Galen, the most famous ancient physician after Hippocrates, was said to be arrogant and claimed miraculous cures. He had a ready explanation for every problem and a reason for every phenomenon—all based upon "scientific" theories. Although Galen wrote nine books on anatomy, seventeen on physiology, six on pathology and thirty on pharmacy, he rarely, if ever, mentioned soul. Not surprisingly, Galen left the healing temple of Asclepius at Pergama and went instead to apply his services among the wealthy in Rome (Garrison, 1929, 112-113).

For fourteen centuries after Galen, European medicine remained practically at a standstill, with any questions relating to disease being referred back to Galen as the final scientific authority from which there could be no appeal. This attitude of "objectivity," exemplified some say by the invention by Leon Battista Alberti in 1435 of "linear perspective vision," prevailed during the Renaissance among physicians such as Vesalius as he dissected the soul-abandoned human body (Romanyshyn, 1989, 65-132). Of course it was Newton likening the human body to a mechanical clock and Descartes postulating complete separation of mind and body that later provided the philosophical underpinnings for the advancement of medical science.

Meanwhile folk medicine or "soul" medicine flourished in the monastic and druidic traditions. A few physicians such as Paracelsus, Nostradamus, Paré, and Mesmer fostered many of these methods. Herbal, midwifery, alchemical, and spiritual practices were usually condemned as superstition by medical societies. Papal edicts and secular laws in Europe usually forced practitioners either to hide their beliefs or risk being persecuted, jailed, or banished.

The Enlightenment, with the empiricism of Roger Bacon and John Locke and the positivism of Berkeley and Hume, promised that anything speculative or metaphysical was not valid and that science was the answer to all of humanity's problems (Bordo, 1987). This set the stage for the advances in technology and science—and the neglect of soul—in our medical practices of today.

And so it is that from our vantage point in the vale of soul, we look up again at the modern ivory tower where liver transplantation is performed. There we find medical science more advanced than ever before. There are electronic computers which can calculate and record data hundreds of times faster than the human brain, imaging machines which can project onto a screen the secrets of the human body, medicines that can block the body's defense mechanism, the rejection of foreign protein. There are surgical tools and techniques beyond the skills of anyone but the most trained doctors, and chemical tests which can accurately measure the concentration of tiny particles of the blood and tissues, the functioning of the delicate and mysterious immune system, and even the arrangements of DNA. All of these advances interact in an environment dedicated to preserving life for those whose diseased livers are incompatible with life. Yet as Hippocrates said, "Desperate diseases require desperate remedies."

In this vast surgical empire, this epitome of science and technology, this crowning achievement of medical therapeutics, what could possibly be missing? Is there *hubris* at work? My mythic sensibility tells me that something is missing. What about soul?

In all this I see shadows. I see a medical treatment in which there are not enough donor organs so that priorities must be made about who will live and who will die. Desperately ill patients must compete with one another for their lives. I see mothers on television pleading for a donor liver and for their own children to have preference over others. I see politics and money favoring the influential in this competition. I see a complex surgical remedy which must compete with treatments for all other maladies for "resource allocation," a process in which doctors in other departments and patients with other ailments question the extensive use of money for liver transplants to the detriment of others who require less expensive treatment and have more hopeful outlooks. I see a system in which government and private insurance companies determine the eligibility of patients for the treatment. I see humans facing a desperate situation in which surgeons tend to offer exaggerated hope and in which, after experiencing the brutality of the operation and prolonged post-operative recuperation, some have regretted that they gave permission for the operation (Knapp, 1998).

Even through the scientific lens of the medical profession, I see shadows. In a 1996 study of the relationship of psychiatric morbidity in organ transplant candidates, over sixty percent of the patients met the criteria for clinical psychological disorders. Nearly twenty-five percent had comorbid clinical disorders (Chacko, 1996, 100-107). Other studies show mixed results as to the efficacy of psychiatric preoperative evaluation for liver transplant candidates (Surman, 1994, 297-307 and Howard, 1994, 643-653). One of the problems is that in many centers the preoperative psychological care of patients undergoing liver transplants was initiated not by the medical professionals but by the insurance companies eager to save money. When they discovered that some of the transplant patients did not comply with postoperative care, and thus their donor livers were rejected, insurance companies faced losing their investment which can exceed three hundred thousand dollars in the first year alone. Not wanting their dollars wasted by poor postoperative compliance, they now demand that psychiatrists try to predict which patients will not be compliant post-operatively. The problems grow from there. Aside from questions about the accuracy of such psychological predictions, the preoperative examiner knows that a diagnosis could deprive the patient of the life saving surgery, creating a tendency to be less than candid that leaves a patient without much needed psychological care (Knapp, 1998).

There are no large-scale, scientifically valid studies of the post-operative emotional reactions to liver transplant surgery, but serious disturbances are not rare. A study of forty adult patients indicated that twenty-four percent were treated for depressive disorders, and others showed medical noncompliance, pain, anxiety, and "organic brain syndrome" (Surman, 1987, 26-31). Psychiatrists have noted that almost all children and adolescents had significant emotional reactions and fantasies concerning having a functioning foreign organ within their own bodies (Knapp, 1998). One adult male identified his female donor with his mother and was unable to psychologically internalize the transplanted liver (Dubovsky, 1979, 1010-1091). Another young man became depressed when he heard that his donor had committed suicide and said that the new liver was living "depressed" inside him. A young woman, whose family had gone against their spiritual beliefs to accept medical treatment, refused to take her immunosuppressive medicines, became sexually promiscuous, and began using illegal drugs after her surgery. Other effects have been documented, such as the development or reversion to eating disorders (Masterson, 1994, 17-21), suicide (Riether, 1994, 574-578), and delirium (Trzepacz, 1988, 3-14). Much more involvement of rehabilitation specialists in the postoperative period is needed (Chong, 1994, 35-43).

The social, religious, aesthetic, and philosophic attitudes (Henderson, 1984) in our culture are perhaps summed up by medical doctor and surgeon Jeff Punch on the University of Michigan Transplant Information Website—"All transplant candidates generally undergo some sort of screening by a psychiatrist or specially trained social worker to make sure that they would be able to handle the routines required after a transplant..." Because of the desperate nature of liver transplant surgery, the psychological care of the patient undergoing this body-altering, anxiety-provoking, spirit-threatening, and soul-splitting procedure seems to be directed primarily toward making sure that the patient's psyche does not get in the way of the success of the operation.

Clearly what is missing in this high-tech medical miracle is soul. Is it not reasonable to assume that any human undergoing a surgical and psychical procedure of this magnitude would have strong emotional reactions to it? Is it not reasonable to know that such an experience would have a profound effect upon an individual's spiritual life? Is it possible that Mickey's addiction to alcohol, like Prometheus' plunder of the gods, was in fact a spiritual emergency (Walsh, 1993, 144-145)? Since twenty percent of liver transplant patients die in the first year and thirty-three percent by the fifth year—and all must someday succumb to death—does not this Promethean labor provide an opportunity for some soul work? Certainly there are many support groups available for transplant patients—the Internet offers eighteen support and informational websites in the United States and an additional nineteen worldwide. There are also numerous books, articles, and local support groups available. Of course it is expected that families and spiritual leaders help.

To be sure, medical professionals try to offer empathy along with their technical skills. But still, what would it be like if we integrated depth psychology into the enterprise of organ transplantation, even as is anesthesia, physical therapy, intensive care, respiratory treatments, and nursing? A consultation with a psychologist costs less than a treatment by a respiratory technician. Including soul in the education and training of health professionals would require more of an attitude change than any additional costs.

We might begin by honoring the organ donor. Except for "harvesting" the organ, the hospital personnel and members of the transplant team offer little regard for the soul of the donor. The twenty year-old lifeguard who donated his liver for Mickey Mantle had saved the life of a drowning man that morning and later in the day provided donor organs for five other patients (Associated Press,

1995). The scientific and technological procedure which was offered to Mickey might have begun with a reverence for the soul of the one who gave the seat of his soul for another, a simple ritual making sacred the organ donor and honoring the spirit-soul-body of the recipient as one might, in turn, bring our healing efforts to the well-being and wholesomeness of all those involved in the patient's care.

The dramatic nature and media exposure of organ transplant surgery elevates its specific cultural symptoms out of shadow and into the light. Remaining in the vale are the shadows of much of the more mundane aspects of medical science. If organ transplant patients are treated without soul, what of the poor, depressed, and elderly individual with an ingrown toenail or the child in an emergency room with a face cut? Psychiatrists have emphasized the need for more emotional care to children and adolescents with serious somatic ailments (Knapp, 1997, 17-23). There is a rapidly increasing national complaint about the loss of soul in medical practice. The rising incidence of malpractice lawsuits, the negative opinions about doctors in public opinion polls and the reported low morale and esteem of doctors and nurses themselves are only a few of the cultural symptoms through which this discontent is expressed.

There is a more positive cultural symptom which asks our attention. It is the rising phenomenon of alternative medicine, practices which revive such ancient techniques as guided imagery, massage, herbal medicines, acupuncture, *I Ching*, body energy therapy, Tui Na, shamanism, spiritual healing, prayer, T'ai Chi Ch'uan, meditation, yoga, kundalini, craniosacral practices, music, art, Alexander techniques, psychoneuroimmunology, Qigong, Rolfing, mindfulness practices, story-telling, and myth. Practitioners of these unscientific healing methods today are ostracized and frowned upon by most of traditional medicine. In a recent study conducted at Stanford University, forty percent of the people randomly polled stated that they had used some form of alternative medicine in the previous year (Astin, 1998, 1548-1553). We might do well to view this trend as a cultural symptom—as "...one of the major political and philosophical statements of our time" (Grossinger, 1990, xii). When soul is excluded from the traditional practice of medicine, it emerges from the shadows as the soul of alternative medicine. Instead of arguing about whether these treatments are scientifically valid, we might better ask what these cultural symptoms are trying to tell us. What is it that people seek when they turn to these forms of treatment? Might it not be a greater sense spirituality and life meaning (Astin, 1998, 1552)?

Alternative medicine departments are springing up in medical centers across the country. These departments usually do not function through the regular medical staff procedures that control traditional medicine but are set aside in the pastoral services department. While the addition of these departments is partly because hospital administrators wish to capitalize on potential revenues, there are small cadres of doctors, administrators, psychologists, pastoral workers, and nurses who believe that soul should be brought back into the mainstream of medicine. There are those who dream that a soulful practice will again become integral to every act in the care of the sick and injured. There are those who imagine that even the most complex scientific and technological advances can be filled with a respect for the mysteries of life—that healing can include mind, body, soul, and spirit.

Bibliography

Achterberg, Jeanne. *Imagery In Healing.* Boston: New American Library, 1985.

Associated Press. Dallas, August 3, 1995—17:24 EDT.

Astin, John A. "Why Patients Use Alternative Medicine." *Journal of the American Medical Association.* 279 (19) May 20, 1998.

Bordo, Susan R. *The Flight To Objectivity.* Albany: State University of New York Press, 1987.

Chacko, Ranjit C. "Relationship of Psychiatric Morbidity and Psychosocial Factors in Organ Transplant Candidates." *Psychosomatics*, Mar-Apr. 1996.

Chambon, Philip. "How Do Animals Heal Themselves?" *Calypso Log: April 1997.* New York: The Cousteau Society, 1997.

Chong, Dennis Khin Hueng. "Rehabilitation of the Patient with Liver Transplantation." *Canadian Journal of Rehabilitation.* 8(1), 1994.

Dubovsky, Steven L. "Problems with Internalization of a Transplanted Liver." *American Journal of Psychiatry.* 1979, 136(8), 1090-1091.

Ellenberger, Henri F. *The Discovery of the Unconscious.* New York: Basic Books, 1970.

Garrison, Fielding H. *History of Medicine.* Philadelphia: W. B. Saunders, 1929.

Grossinger, Richard. *Planet Medicine.* Berkeley: North Atlantic Books, 1990.

Henderson, Joseph L. *Cultural Attitudes in Psychological Perspective.* Toronto: Inner City Books, 1984.

Hillman, James. "Peaks and Vales," *Spring*, 1979.

Howard, Louise, M. "The Psychiatric Assessment of Liver Transplant Patients with Alcoholic Disease." *Journal of Psychosomatic Medicine*, 38(7), 1994.

Knapp, Penelope. "Consultation Liaison in Child Psychiatry." *Journal of the American Academy of Child and Adolescent Psychiatry*, 37(1), 1997.

_______________. Professor of Psychiatry, University of California at Davis. Personal Communication, 1998.

Masterson, Brian J. "Anorexia Nervosa and Alcoholism in a Female Liver Transplant Recipient." *Eating Disorders: The Journal of Treatment and Prevention.* Spring, 2(1), 1994.

Punch, Jeff. http://www.med.umich.edu/trans/transweb/asktw/answers, 1996.

Reither, Anne Marie (1994). "Suicide in Liver Transplant Patients." *Psychosomatics.* 35(6), 1994.

Romanyshyn, Robert. *Technology as Symptom and Dream.* London: Routledge, 1989.

Slater, Glen. "Re-Sink The Titanic." *Spring 62*, 1998.

Surman, Robert. "Psychosomatic Aspects of Liver Transplantation." *Psychotherapy and Psychosomatics.* 48(1-4), 1987.

Surman, Owen S. "Psychiatric Aspects of Liver Transplantation." *Psychosomatics.* May-Jun 35(3) 1994.

Trzepacz, Paula T. "Delirium in Liver Transplantation Candidates." *Biological Psychiatry.* 24(1), 1988.

United Network for Organ Sharing, (UNOS) Richmond, Vir., *Annual Report*, 1996.

Walsh, R. *Paths Beyond Ego.* New York: G. P. Putnam's Sons, 1993.

Technology and Non-efficient Practices

MICHAEL STAPLES

> Within and beyond the looming presence of modern technology there dawns the possibility of a fuller relationship between man and Being—and hence between man and all that is—than there has ever been.[1]

The technological way of seeing the world often brings about significant distress. It can strip soul from us, pushing up rates of depression. Often referred to as the pathology of the twentieth century, one of the most common forms of depression in our culture, known as Dysthymia, refers to a loss of soul, to the essence that defines who each of us "is."[2] In this sense, freeing our relation to technology means finding a way to affirm our technological devices, while at the same time denying the technological way of seeing the world that strips away the essence of who we are. To better understand the meaning of a "free" relation to technology

[1] Martin Heidegger, *The Question Concerning Technology and Other Essays* (New York: Harper & Row, 1977).

[2] The thymus gland was one of several ancient "seats"of the soul. Depression was thought to be caused by the loss of soul from its seat within this region.

Michael Staples attended Pacifica Graduate Institute and now works with the Center for Intersubjective Studies in Sonoma, California. He presented a version of this paper in 1998 at the Winter Institute of Medical Physics in Colorado Springs, Colorado.

and distinguish it from the kind of relation in which we are driven by the needs of efficiency and optimization, it may be best to contrast two senses of technology—the first as a way of seeing the world, and the second, the local manifestations derived from this way of seeing the world. We tend to miss this distinction when we think of technology only in terms of its scholastic definition—a means to an end. This definition is not incorrect. On the contrary, it is so correct that it tends to focus our attention only on technologies of a local nature, obscuring the technological way of seeing the world that has us in its grip. But it is this essence of technology that calls for more and more flexibility, more and more efficiency, shaping our way of seeing the world by focusing our vision on the maximum yield for the minimum expense.

Everything, everywhere—people, trees, oceans—are called to stand-by for further ordering.[3] A forest of old-growth trees is seen as a potential profit center. A desert is seen as a potential for irrigation improvements. People are seen as human resourcesor they are often not seen at all. What is missed by defining technology as a means to an end, is that this way of seeing the world as a thing to be ordered is entirely new in the development of humanity's understanding.

One can distinguish, as philosopher Martin Heidegger did in the early part of this century, alternatives to our modern way of understanding the world. Early on, people understood the world in terms of *physis* (the Greek root of physics). The things of the world emerged spontaneously as objects set over against humanity's subjectivity. At another time, humans understood the world through a paradigm that defined beings as creatures of a creator God.[4] The technological attitude we hold today came about slowly, ushered in by Galileo and Descartes, then carried on by Newton's physics and the philosophy of John Locke and Leibnitz. But it was not until this century that we have been able to see the effects. Albert Gormann writes that before the triumph of technological devices,

---

[3] Hubert L. Dreyfus, *Gaining a Free Relation to Technology* (University of California at Berkeley: Conference Recording Service. 9/8, 1994). Applied Heidegger Conference. Living with Technology Symposium.

[4] Hubert L. Dreyfus, and Charles Spinosa, "Highway Bridges and Feasts: Heidegger and Borgmann on How to Affirm Technology" (Berkeley: University of California, Undated Paper).

> ...people primarily engaged in practices that nurtured or crafted various things. So gardeners developed the skills and put in the effort necessary for nurturing plants, musicians acquired the skill necessary for music...[but technology]...replaces the worlds of poiesis, craftsmen, and Christians with a world in which subjects control objects. In such a world the things that call for nurturing, craftsmanly, or praising practices are replaced by devices that offer a more and more transparent or commodious way of satisfying a desire.[5]

Heidegger, too, questioned the quality of life of one living in the shared understanding of modern technology:

> [One]...is regularly expected, and expects himself, to be able to impose order on all data, to process every sort of entity, nonhuman and human alike, and to devise solutions for every kind of problem. He is forever getting things under control.[6]

Those disposed of by society when they are no longer valued comprise just one group placed under distress by this mode of thought. There are others, carved into our lives as technology demands that everything and everyone everywhere stand ready to be used as a resource, ready to be optimized. But when this happens, neither people nor things are understood to have an essence, to have an identity, or even to have the goal of satisfying their own arbitrary desires.[7] Hubert Dreyfus speaks directly to this issue:

> If the computer paradigm becomes so strong that people begin to think of themselves as digital devices on the model of work in artificial intelligence, then, since for the reasons we have been rehearsing, machines cannot be like human beings, human beings may become progressively like machines. During the past two thousand years the importance of objectivity; the belief that actions are governed by fixed values; the notion that skills can be formalized; and in general that one can have a theory of practical activity, have gradually exerted their influence in psychology and in social science. People have begun to think of themselves as objects able to fit into the inflexible calculations of disembodied machines...

[5] Dreyfus and Spinosa, *op. cit.*

[6] Martin Heidegger, *op. cit.*

[7] Dreyfus and Spinosa, *op. cit.*

> Our risk is not the advent of superintelligent computers,
> but of subintelligent human beings.[8]

These are problems that linger in the shadows of consciousness, arise from the depths of our shared background and know-how, and shape our thoughts. So close, so much a part of our indeterminate common sense, it is invisible to us. One example of a shared background is the acceptable distance held between people in social contexts. This distance varies in different cultures, and it is not taught explicitly. Instead, it is part of a shared background of understanding. An example related specifically to American and European cultures is the way we understand the quantity "more" in terms of the spacial schema of "up." Prices go up. The number of books published each year rise. Gross earnings fall.[9] These examples illustrate that no experience exists in isolation. The experience we have of someone standing too close or too far away is embedded within a background we share with others. The orientation of "more" as "up" is embedded within a background of common experiences (e.g., if you add more liquid to a container, the level goes up). In fact, perceiving anything at all involves perceiving it as embedded within a whole we share with others—experiences that in general rely on a context of meaning which is often neither entirely conscious nor entirely unconscious.

Edgar Rubin, the author of the first book on the phenomenon of figure and ground, gave several examples in which visual figure-ground situations were ambiguous and therefore reversible. This visual experience can be used as a metaphor for experience in general. The familiar picture of a goblet which can be also perceived as two profiled faces confronting each other is a good example. "When one sees the goblet, the outlines look so completely different from those of the faces that the identity can only be understood intellectually, not acknowledged visually."[10] But the two images represented in the picture cannot be seen at the same time. This is significant because it implies an unconscious (for lack of a better term) background dynamically related to our immediate awareness of foreground.

[8] Hubert L. Dreyfus, *What Computers Still Can't Do: A Critique of Artificial Reason* (Cambridge, Mass.: MIT Press, 1997), 280.

[9] Mark Johnson, *The Body in the Mind* (Chicago: The University of Chicago Press, 1987).

[10] Rudolf Arnheim, *Art and Visual Perception: A Psychology of the Creative Eye* (Los Angeles: University of California Press, 1974), 225.

There is a tradition that presents a strict dichotomy between subject and object, foreground and background, soul and matter, conscious and unconscious, reaching into antiquity.[11] On one count, self-contained objects are seen in terms of "figure" against an empty or otherwise qualitatively different space which serves as "ground." Rutherford and Bohr's traditional model of atomic structure is an example. "Notice," writes Rudolph Arnheim,

> how the peculiar blend of discomfort and elation which one experiences when such a system is redefined as a continuous electro-magnetic field, in which the objects or particles may be thought of according to Erwin Schrodinger, as 'more or less temporary entities within the wave field, whose form and general behavior are nevertheless so clearly and sharply determined by the laws of waves that many processes take place as if these temporary entities were substantial permanent beings.[12]

We can push the model of visual perception further, past the immediate process of informing us about how far to stand away from people, to a general analogy of how background contexts shape our understanding of what it is to be a person or object.

This indeterminate background understanding is one of those things computers cannot seem to master. They cannot know how far to stand from someone unless they are connected to a programmer equipped with the shared background of understanding, and they are provided with some form of "body." But even with programming they cannot know how far to stand from someone in a given social context because this sort of know-how is indeterminate and the computer can only work with determinant data.

Hubert Dreyfus tells of an early attempt to use neuronets to teach a computer to distinguish between two pictures: one of a forest of trees with military tanks and one of a forest of trees without tanks.

---

[11] "Freud's conception of the Id and the Ego retains essential features of the ancient model. The Id is the central source of blindly radiating energy. Under the impact of the physical environment, the outer sheath of the psyche develops the organs of sensory perception and becomes a protective bark against injuries from the outside... None of these conceptions transcends the basic perceptual pattern of figure and ground." Rudolf Arnheim, *Visual Thinking* (1969).

[12] Rudolf Arnheim, *Visual Thinking* (Berkeley: University of California Press, 1969), 286.

The researchers were able to teach the computer to distinguish between the two pictures, and the Army was delighted. But just to make sure, the researchers took another set of pictures of the same two scenes, and this time the computer could not tell the difference. Why? Eventually the research team figured out that the difference between the pictures was that some were taken on a sunny day while others were taken on a cloudy day, and what the computer was learning to distinguish was not the difference between tanks and no tanks but shadows and no shadows.[13]

This story reveals the issue of recognizing significance which is one thing computers have not been able to handle on their own.[14] Much of the efficiency enhancing software coming onto the market today is often viewed by physicists as a threat to their job security (yet another example of the anxiety associated with technology). But it should not be, because the one thing we cannot infuse the computer with is the ability to distinguish significance—a product of the shared background of understanding. It is the product of the indeterminate background defining the determinant foreground. There is no computer substitute for it. As a result, the computer can help to supply and order facts but remains unable to see relevance.

It would be pointless to conclude that technology is bad or evil and must be romantically eradicated from our culture. On the contrary, technology is something we depend upon in a positive sense. The question then—and this returns us to the issue of gaining a free relation to technology—asks how we can keep our technological devices without offering ourselves over as just another resource to be optimized. An initial answer would perhaps see technology as being our latest shared understanding of the world, thus bringing the background understanding forward into view. Bringing into the foreground of awareness is the first move toward gaining a freedom toward technology. From a depth psychologist's point of view, bringing unconscious "material" forward into consciousness is an important step in opening oneself to a free relation to background phenomena (unconscious material or practices). In this case perhaps that is the most we can do, for theoretically we can never extract ourselves from our shared back-

[13] Hubert L. Dreyfus, 1994, *op. cit.*
[14] *Ibid.*

ground.[15] However, by opening ourselves to the awareness of our relation to it, we alter our degree of freedom with respect to it.

Bringing background understanding forward would move us in the direction of neither pushing technology as our only goal nor resisting it. It would mean keeping clear about where we fit into the picture,[16] cultivating the awareness that what is most important in our lives is not necessarily subject to efficient enhancement but may lie instead within the practices typically pushed out by efficiency. Non-efficient practices like friendship, skiing, or love hold up to us the alternatives to the technological thinking that must optimize for optimization's sake, that must turn the world into a resource to be endlessly ordered. Valuing non-efficient practices frees our relation to the technological attitude in which we are embedded, opening us to ways of affirming our technological devices, while at the same time denying the technological way of seeing the world associated with them that would deny the essence of who we are.

---

[15] Hubert L. Dreyfus, *Being-in-the-World: A Commentary on Heidegger's Being and Time*, Division I (Cambridge, Mass.: MIT Press, 1991).

[16] Theoretically we can never extract ourselves from the shared background of understanding. We can never stand outside it and look back upon it. (i.e. we can never objectify it). We are always in it, involved with it. The most we can do is cultivate an awareness of our position within it, dealing with this position hermeneutically.

The Last Hour: When a Therapist Retires

ANN C. SMITH

I was one of those people who never dreamed of retiring, much less at age fifty-nine. I was happy with my life and the way I spent my time. My work played a central role in the richness of my life. When I thought about getting older, I envisioned working at least fifteen or so clinical hours each week for as long as I lived. Back then I felt that I was in my prime, and I woke up almost every day full of enthusiasm for seeing the usual nine or ten patients, plus consultants, for the day. Probably the only time I ever thought of retirement was at the end of each tax year when my accountant dutifully reminded me to transfer money into my Keogh account.

I remember the fiftieth birthday party I gave for friends and colleagues at my new home in the hills. That fifty year marker did not signify to me a time of beginning to "wind-down;" rather, I celebrated entering the prime of life. As I stood in the warm air on the curved wooden deck overlooking the bay I thought to myself, "Now everything is in place. Now, not only can I fully enjoy everything I have worked for to this point, but also I can move smoothly into the best and most productive years of my life."

Ann C. Smith holds a doctorate in psychology and practiced psychotherapy for twenty-seven years. She lives in Berkeley, California, where she writes and volunteers with the elderly and the homeless.

At the time I taught in a graduate program, supervised clinicians in training, and did some writing. But the core of my life's work was the fifty to sixty hours of intensive psychotherapy with clients each week. Trainees and sometimes even other therapists used to ask me, "How do you work so many hours and see so many patients?" My answer was that I loved the work and it was energizing rather than draining. The process gave me experiences from which I grew professionally, and I gained an ever deepening understanding of what it is to be human. My satisfaction with my work also enriched my personal life. I was committed to a long-term relationship with someone I loved. I had raised a child who was away at a university pursuing a passion for theater. My partner and I each seemed to have energy, robust health, and bright futures. My fiftieth year marker told of a journey that was going well.

I do not mean to give the impression that my journey in life had been entirely smooth or blissful. Along the way I had experienced losses and disappointments. Both my parents died early. A first love had died. An affair which I hoped would lead to marriage proved ill- chosen. One of my patients committed suicide early in my career. I wrote a book but could not find a publisher. A long period of soul-searching included a seven-year analysis. Yet through it all, I had never doubted that I was on the right path, and along the way the world confirmed my confidence and convictions. The career opportunities came, the friends and the love came, the patients came, the money and prestige came—the blessings, both inner and outer, were abundant and freely bestowed. Little did I know on that spring-like evening, standing with a host of good friends beside a loaded buffet table, champagne glass in hand, celebrating a milestone of good health and good fortune, that less than nine years later, I was to be forced into early retirement and into an unchosen detour through the depths of a psychological and spiritual struggle with loss, illness, and mortality.

In my fifty-ninth year I suffered two mild strokes which left me physically unchanged but cognitively and emotionally altered forever. I experienced losses of memory and mental organization. Almost overnight, work that had been easy required an immense effort—to remember, to concentrate, and at times even to be fully present. For twenty-seven years I had been one of those therapists who remembers everything—details of a patient's history, current life, our interactions in recent hours, important themes from hours long past—everything. I took only the barest of notes and seldom needed to refer to them. In contrast after the strokes, I feverishly wrote and reviewed case notes during the ten minutes between patients and still sometimes got things wrong. I was slowly losing my confidence. I began to lose sleep at night worrying about real or imagined mistakes I had made. Gradually, I became aware of growing tense. I became more and more exhausted.

Eventually it became clear to that I needed to think about cutting back my hours or even stopping my work. I went into psychotherapy and hired a consultant to help me deal with the issues involved in making such a decision and, if necessary, carrying it out. With the therapist I probed the psychological meanings that stopping work and closing my practice would have for me. With the consultant, I discussed the clinical issues and used her to help me stay on track week to week in my work with my patients.

At first I entertained the idea of continuing work with just a few patients. However, it soon became clear to me that this was not an option. Only four or five patients were nearing readiness for termination. What of the others? Certainly I could not tell some patients that I would be continuing a small practice, but they would not be included in it. After looking at all of the alternatives, I knew that I must begin to prepare all of my patients for termination and eventually close my practice. On the night that I made my final decision, before I got into bed, I fell on my knees and begged God to give my life back to me. I pleaded and bargained with Him to be able to continue my work and my life as I had known it.

I had made my decision and was preparing to act on it, but I was a long way from surrendering to my fate. Before announcing my retirement, I decided not to tell my patients that I was retiring because of a stroke. I felt that since I was not severely ill, I need not burden my patients with the disclosure of the reasons why I was retiring. It was on a crisp September morning as the days were beginning to grow short, and an autumn wind was starting to blow the gold and orange leaves from the branches of the tree outside my office window, that I told the first patient that I would be retiring in a few months.

I knew of some professionals who had retired at sixty or earlier. My dentist, my internist, and my veterinarian, all only slightly older than me, had retired. However, I knew of only one therapist of any age who had retired. Therapists never seem to retire. Perhaps this was one reason why the discovery that I needed to retire came as such a blow. The news was equally a shock to many of my patients who could not understand why a therapist would retire in middle age. In fact, I had seldom heard therapists even talk about retirement. It almost seems that the silence about retiring, particularly the silence about the possibility of needing to retire, is part of a belief that the therapist will be there forever. However, this silence is viewed, it would seem to involve a denial of frailty, illness, or vulnerability, and perhaps in its extreme, an avoidance of facing mortality.

In addition, the scarcity of literature on the subject, as cited in the PsychINFO database, suggests that surprisingly little has been written about therapist retirement or therapist illness. In fact, psychotherapists and psychologists are the most neglected groups in retirement literature. I found little about the psychologist who retires and closes a private practice, and almost nothing about the psychotherapist who is forced to retire because of declining health or cognitive abilities. I did find one article dealing with countertransference issues when the therapist is ill or disabled.[1] Also, there were only a few articles[2] written by therapists thinking ahead about life after retirement. One survey article[3] dealing with psychiatrist retirement and age-related impairment showed that only fifty-three percent anticipated retiring by age seventy, and 13.5 percent reported that they planned to practice psychotherapy until death. Thus, little light has been shed along the way for the therapist who retires, particularly when retirement is due to declining health.

A number of times after deciding to retire, I thought back to another loss and period of adjustment which I had experienced fifteen years earlier. I had been a long distance runner for many years and

[1] P. A. Dewald, "Countertransference Issues When the Therapist is Ill or Disabled," *American Journal of Psychotherapy*, Spring, 1994, 48(2), 221-230.

[2] One is Maria Julia, Keith M. Kilty, and Virginia Richardson, "Social Worker Preparedness for Retirement: Gender and Ethnic Considerations," *Social Work*, Sept. 1995, 40 (5), 610-620. Another is F. M. Baker, Bruce H. Warren, JoLynn Muraida, and Gerard Muraida. "A Survey of Retirement Planning by Texas Psychiatrists," *Journal of Geriatric Psychiatry and Neurology*, Jan.-Mar. 1993, 6(1), 14-19.

[3] James D. Guy, Miriam J. Stark, Paul Poelstra, and Janet K. Souder, "Psychotherapist Retirement and Age-related Impairment: Results of a National Survey," *Psychotherapy*, Winter 1987, 24(4), 816-820.

had loved running, physically, psychologically, and spiritually. I could hardly imagine the day would come when I would no longer be getting up before sunrise six days a week to spend an hour running on dirt trails strewn with pine needles. But, in my fortieth year, after running several marathon races and feeling still in my prime, I was shocked when one morning, after covering only two or three miles, a heavy leaden pain ran down my left leg. Within seconds my left ankle and foot were numb. A degenerative disc problem was diagnosed, and I underwent a lamonectomy. I tried to resume my running after recovering from the surgery. Day after day I would start out, and each time after less than a mile my leg gave out, and I stumbled to the dirt beneath my feet. I grieved for the loss of this part of my life. Now having to give up the work that was the center of my life was like that, only harder.

Premature retirement had many meanings for me. Giving up the work I loved after twenty-five years meant, first and foremost, that my vocation would no longer continue to be the significant source of purpose that it had been. In my worst moments I thought of my impending retirement as the end of the road. It was hard to imagine that other meaningful possibilities would open up. I was also sometimes angry about what was happening to me and to my well-planned life. During this time I found the laments of some of the *Psalms* quite helpful in giving expression to my emotions, such as *Psalm* 102: 23-24: "He has brought down my strength before my time; he has shortened the number of my days. And I said, 'O my God, do not take me away in the midst of my days.'" There were moments when I found myself suddenly less patient with people and situations that had never ruffled me before. At other times I felt rising frustration at what I perceived as obstacles. I worked hard to be able to feel, but not to be ruled by, either anger or despair. It was important for me to be able to integrate these feelings not only for my own health, but also in order to have the distance which would keep me from communicating these feelings to my patients.

At the end of a full week of telling my patients of my decision to retire, I realized that I had prepared myself more for expressions of anger when most people expressed shock and sadness. Several people choked up with emotion, and some shed tears. Many said that it had never occurred to them that I might retire since I seemed to be in my prime. One person put it poignantly when she said it never occurred to her that I might leave her. Three patients expressed their feeling of loss by saying that it was like losing a mother or a father. I was moved by the openness and vulnerability of many of the responses.

By the end of the week, I felt unusually fatigued and emotionally exhausted. Tears rolled silently down my cheeks as I drove home in my car on a rainy Friday night. I had done my best—I had done good work and had continued to do good work throughout that week of telling my patients that I was leaving. But I surrendered to the sadness. I felt a loss and how much I cared for the people who had been my patients. I not only felt compassion for their loss but also for the extent of my own loss and how much I would miss the work.

The next week after more fully realizing the immensity of the impending loss, I was especially happy to be back in my office seeing patients. From then on the time remaining seemed incredibly precious and alive, and I fell in love with my work all over again. It was almost like going back to the days before the first stroke. There were days when I felt almost as I had when I was ten years younger; I had greeted the dawn with an abundant reserve, spent a little time in meditation, showered, and went off to work as to a wedding feast. I had indeed been given a renewed appreciation for life. I still remember the clarity of the mornings before I retired; the clear cold February air and the winter light; my internal state was a mixture of heightened awareness and eagerness for the day's work ahead and a calm sad stillness. Despite the sadness, I felt content and happy because I knew I was giving my best in this last phase of clinical work—and that it was good. It was like running a marathon. All of my effort went into making the last mile as strong and good as the previous twenty-five had been.

I found that I did not look forward to endless days of rest and leisure to do with as I wished, as friends and a doctor had prescribed. I began to recognize with clarity that I would not be able to feel content and fulfilled living a life of leisure. At that time I had no idea what I would turn my attention to, but I knew that I would have to find some pursuit to which I could devote my heart and use the resources and talents I had left.

I discovered first hand some of the issues that are tied up in work and the loss of work. So much of American culture revolves around striving, succeeding, and making money. Much of this seems individualistic and external, but on another level work binds one to the world and to life. Even Kahlil Gibran once wrote:

> You work that you may keep pace with the earth and the soul of the earth. For to be idle is to become a stranger unto the seasons, and to step out of life's process, that marches in majesty and proud submission towards the infinite... And when you work with love you bind yourself to yourself, and to one another, and to God.[4]

There is also fundamental need to contribute to life and to make a difference.

My work had been for me a vocation, and there were spiritual issues involved in giving it up. I found that I needed to re-work the basis of my faith in order to deal with the loss of the cultural and archetypal gods I had erected in conjunction with my work. Dealing with the psychological issues alone was not enough. I could no longer be the favored daughter who carried the torch forward. I needed to rediscover a faith in God based in enduring, unconditional worth, which no modern therapeutic approach alone could give me. During this time I began working with a spiritual director who reminded me at the end of our first meeting of the scriptural passage *John* 12:24: "Very truly, I tell you, unless a grain of wheat falls into the earth and dies, it remains just a single grain; but if it dies, it bears much fruit." My old way of life would have to die, and I would have to surrender in order to give birth to a part of me that would perhaps bear new fruit, the nature of which I could not yet imagine.

As I approached the last few weeks of practice, I had begun to make peace with my decision although the grieving process was far from ended. I believed that I was doing the right thing for myself, and also for my patients, since I knew I could no longer continue to give them my best. It was time for me to leave them, and for my patients to go on and live their lives and, if they chose, to continue their therapy with someone else.

In the last month or so, the phone rang often with an old friend or colleague calling to make plans for dinner or lunch together to honor and celebrate my retirement. A number of former patients

---

[4] Kahlil Gibran, *The Prophet* (New York: Alfred A. Knopf, 1956).

who had heard of my impending retirement wanted to return for one or two sessions before I closed my practice. Those were busy weeks. It was a chance to review work done not only with current patients but also with patients from different eras in my practice of over twenty-five years—and, of saying good-bye to them all.

Some of the patients I had known for years had trouble dealing with my retirement, and our remaining sessions were often spent exploring their difficulties. Greg, for instance, with whom I had worked on and off for many years, was unwilling to let our professional relationship go. I had watched him mature, embark on a profession, marry, have children, and bury his mother. In the last month of our work, his voice was hoarse and broken with emotion, and his eyes brimmed with tears as he told me that he could not bear the thought that he would never be in touch with me again after all these years and would not be able to call me when his aging father died. When he finished speaking he sat with downcast eyes, and I asked, "Why not? Why can't you call me if you want to?" I felt it would be inhuman to refuse contact to this patient.

Joane's mother had frequently attacked her first female child verbally. Joane's primary fear throughout our work was that someday for some reason I would see her as she really was and would hate her. When I told her I was leaving, she became afraid that I would hate her now if she dared be angry about my leaving. Eventually she expressed to me the hurt and anger which had always brought on her mother's rage and condemnation. She was overcome by sobs and later by joy to discover that my response was not hatred or anger but compassion and understanding.

Irene, upon hearing of my retirement, became immediately convinced that I was dying of a terminal illness. When Irene was eleven her mother died of a progressive illness, and Irene's father had blamed her for her mother's illness. Now Irene was afraid that she had somehow made me sick, too, through being needy. I reminded her that she had been made to feel that her natural expression of need as a child had somehow been bad or destructive, and that she was afraid that was the situation with me. I told her on the contrary that I was not dying, and furthermore that she had added to my life not detracted from it. In the next session she said that suddenly the fact of my leaving no longer felt bad. She went on in the remaining weeks to consolidate her progress in therapy and to experience a new feeling of joy and freedom.

Like Joane, Deborah had been the primary object of her mother's hostile projections but had few compensatory "good objects." She had married rejecting men; friends had abandoned her; individual therapy in the past had ended in virtual rejection; she had become the scapegoat in a therapy group. Her work with me had its ups and downs, but gradually she had begun to internalize a new and more positive image of herself, made better friends, and married a more stable and loving man. When I announced my retirement, the old issues returned. She believed that I was tired of working with her and found her too difficult. Furthermore, she feared that I was terminating with her and continuing with other, more valued patients. I told her that this was not the situation, that I was leaving my practice completely and would not be continuing with anyone. I also told her I felt that we had developed a good relationship which I enjoyed. I said she deserved someone good with whom to continue her work and that I would help her in this if she wished. A card she later wrote affirmed my feeling that she left knowing that I cared about her, and that I had been moved by the suffering in her struggle and rejoiced in her happiness.

Eva's image of herself as she told it to me early in the therapy was of a three-dimensional sealed box floating in space with no support and no connection. Embedded in our work had been her need for, and fear of, connectedness. I waited patiently and supportively for her to begin to feel safe, and eventually she began first to refer to me as her "reference point" and later to seek engagement. Soon after I announced my retirement she reported a dream about being orphaned which she associated with being forgotten or disconnected. She said later that the separation from me would be easier for her if, after I left, she could "place me somewhere in the world," just to know that I was out there and had not faded away or disappeared. I told her that I would be staying in the area (unlike her father, who disappeared when she was nine). She seemed calmed and comforted by this knowledge. In the next to last hour, she gave me a prose poem in which she compared her relationship with me to the way she now felt about her keys—which she had lost many times. If she misplaced her keys momentarily, she now trusted that they were still there where she had left them and that she would remember and find them again when she needed them. In the last hour she said she hoped that she would still be findable in my old appointment books years from now. I said in parting that I would indeed remember her fondly.

Early in her life Gwen had felt pushed to go out on her own prematurely and without enough support. In the first year of therapy, she told of giving up and putting aside, at age three, a soft piece of fur which she had often held against her cheek for comfort. This memory became a metaphor in much of her therapeutic work. Her mother, who had never really been emotionally available, had died when Gwen was thirteen. When I told her of my retirement, she became tearful, and then said her mind was a blank and there was no further point in talking about anything. Over time, with my encouragement, she was able to talk about how hard it was for her to lose our relationship when she was not ready to go out on her own, feelings she had never been able to articulate or express with her parents. In the last week she reported a dream in which she found valuable things her mother had left for her after she had died. She also said a friend was starting a group for "motherless daughters" and that she planned to join it. In our last session I told her that she was dear to me, and I would be with her in spirit.

Ken's initial response to my announcement that I was retiring was to be happy for me and to wish me well. He said the timing was okay for him because he felt he had nearly completed his therapeutic work and was about ready to terminate. Later he acknowledged disappointment and some anger that he had not been able to be the one to make the decision about when his therapy would end. He also talked about his fantasy of taking control and leaving without saying good-bye as he tended to do in previous relationships. At his last session, Ken came bearing a vase of beautiful spring flowers. He was awkward and halting as he tried to stay with the moment and talk about the gratitude and love he was feeling. He said this was the first time in his life he had not run away from saying good-bye, adding that he hoped he would be similarly available to say good-bye to his parents when the time came for their deaths.

I came across an announcement for a three-day retreat to be held at a convent nearby scheduled for the weekend before what would be my final week of work. I mailed the registration form immediately.

The retreat felt right for me at that time, and I thought my noticing the announcement was a bit of synchronicity not to be bypassed. I felt it would help me prepare to be present, available, and at my best as a therapist during a week of endings and good-byes. That last week would not only require my best therapeutic skills but also call upon me as a person. On the Sunday night I returned from the retreat, I prayed that my presence and my work during the coming week would be a blessing to my patients, one they would take away with them forever.

In that final week, my eyes as well as my patients' eyes were often moist. Along with the spoken expressions of gratitude and sadness and love, there were cards with messages saying what the therapy had meant, poetry, and gifts of flowers, music, and art. Words were spoken and exchanged that, all too often are spoken only at a wake or memorial service when one of the two persons is no longer there to receive and respond. On the last night of the last week, I did as I had always done—except it was for the last time. I saw my last patient and made the last entry in my case notebook. For the last time I put on my coat and turned out the light. I closed the door, walked down the stairs, got in my car, and drove away.

Myths Not to Live By: A Book Review

SHEILA GRIMALDI-CRAIG

Robert Elwood. *The Politics of Myth: A Study of C. G. Jung, Mircea Eliade, and Joseph Campbell.* Albany: State University of New York Press, 1999. Pp. 207. Paper, $17.95.

The therapeutic uses of myth were the essence of Jung's analytical psychology. I say "were" only because so many people have passed on to their own eclectic versions and practices, some still very mythy, like archetypal imagining and soul psychology—pretty much where this journal stands—but others less so, like the radical dreaming people and the new shamanists of various selfhoods, and some even to a replacement of the Jungian or the Hillmanian altogether via the logics of Hegel. The fact is, as Freud repudiated myths and religions, Jung embraced them. Myth was Jung's way out of the modern world and the way back to...what?

"Mass man," as he was called back then, was the invention of the Industrial Revolution, the French Revolution, and all the ideological revolutions to come. Mass man was soulless, spiritless, rootless, an urban zombie of despair and meaninglessness and materialism. Mass man was at his worst in Communist and Fascist countries, but in

Sheila Grimaldi-Craig is the regular book reviewer for this journal. Her first book, *The Pleasures of Recluses*, will be published in 2001 by Spring.

Jung's eyes even the capitalist United States was prey. In all this Jung was far from alone—virtually all post-World War I intellectuals, from Ortega y Gasset to T. S. Eliot, from Gershom Scholem to Ernst Cassirer, felt the same way. Dr. Jung's prescription for mass man's (and more often mass woman's) ills was a dose of genuine spirits of myth; there are ample testimonies that it worked and still works very well, thank you—and as long as there are, wholesale criticism of Jungian thought is as pointless as criticism of vitamin supplements used to be. You know which side I am on.

But in the past few years, and with mounting volume, the shadow side of Jung and Jungianism has been, to put it mildly, under scrutiny. Surely it behooves everyone who even remotely dabbles in such matters—anyone, that is, who would even begin to take myth seriously as a prescriptive of life—to be aware of just how ugly that shadow could get. *The Politics of Myth* is a good place to start. It is well written (if absurdly un-proofread by the author and the State University of New York Press), fair to restrained in its judgments and judgmentalness—an important criterion—and knowledgeable in the ways of myth work and religion theory. Author Robert Elwood is Professor of Religion Emeritus at the University of Southern California and a former student of Mircea Eliade. His is the voice of a veteran of the culture wars of the past half century, at least as they were fought in the religion departments of academe. Two of his previous books were *The Sixties Spiritual Awakening* and *The Fifties Spiritual Marketplace*, neither of which have I read but both of which, by their titles, suggest the venue of his field of combat.

For Elwood the heart of the problem or the core of this Shadow was a paradox: in the dialectic of myth in this century, the tribal collective consciousness that was so esteemed at first by virtually all of Europe's mythologists—and in which the individual, as hero, was supposed to win triumphs on behalf of all for a dimension that was supposed to be larger than the individual self—became the thing they all hated, namely, mass man. In this environment it became impossible and dispiriting for the hero to win anything larger than himself that was worthwhile. "The paradox of collective and heroic in myth," Elwood writes, "was never fully resolved" (28). Instead, we got either individual psychological procedures, hardly altruistic, or the horrors of nationalism.

"These two processes," he writes, "the individual psychological and the nationalistic, were ostensibly at odds with the fundamental character of modern society—its scientific, 'statistical' homogenization, its professedly democratic institutions" (30). So the mythology movement inevitably became political (always denying it, of course) and not liberal or progressively political—that would only add fuel to the mass fire—but conservative and sometimes even fascist.

Elwood continues,

> But here is where the approach of the mythologists needs to be set carefully against the strand of thought which led to Mussolini, Hitler, and Stalin. In fact, the gnostic mythology of Jung, Eliade and Campbell, contemplative in fundamental intent, contrasts significantly with the apocalyptic definition and use of myth in the political wing of modern mythology. In the end, Jung, Eliade, and Campbell turn out to be more oriented toward individual than national transformation, though no less significantly political for that reason. (30)

While all three mythologists romanticized myth into a fantasy of cosmic purity—with the oldest myths being freshest from the hands of the gods—and also romanticized history into something bad, a fall or decline—in the end they internalized myth "as a means of cohesion with one's own true self rather than with soil and social movements" (35).

Thus, they saved myth for what Elwood calls "the inward therapeutic," a process that is still the essence of all forms of analytical psychology. But at what a price, and how far all three men finally came from their original positions! It seems even farther today, for us, because we see not only the early background of anti-Semitism, theirs and their countrymen's, but also the climax of that prejudice in the Holocaust. They saw that, too, in their lifetimes. But today that prejudice, like all racist prejudices, seems so transparent that those of us who admire their work rather naïvely gasp in amazement—or cluck with disdain if we do not—that men of such great insight into religious thought could have been so possessed by it. Today with facility we see it as Shadow projection, forgetting where and how and with whom the very notion of Shadow psychology first appeared in our discourse.

In 1934, in "The State of Psychotherapy Today," (*CW 10*, § 353) a paper Elwood cites, Jung wrote notoriously of Jews: "The Jew, who is something of a nomad, has never yet created a cultural form of his own and as far as we can see never will, since all his instincts and talents require a more or less civilized nation to act as a host for their development." And that Jews "have in common with women being physically weaker, they have to aim at chinks in the armor of their opponents[adversary]...having a civilization twice as old, they are vastly more conscious than we of human weaknesses..." (63). He claimed he was not intending to be anti-Semitic. Certainly on a personal level he was not. With friends ranging from Erich Neumann to his personal secretary Aniela Jaffé, not to mention Freud himself, such a charge would be absurd. But he seems to have gotten only deeper into the mess. In a letter to Gerhard Adler, which Elwood cites, Jung wrote: "So when I criticize Freud's Jewishness I am not criticizing the *Jews* but rather that damnable capacity of the Jew, as exemplified by Freud, to deny his own nature" (64).

Elwood comments that "the sweeping, unqualified manner in which Jung applied various attitudes to Aryans and Jews as such suggests the extent to which he was prepared to think only in terms of the collective unconscious when dealing with social and political matters and not with individual differences. Closely connected to this capacity is Jung's obvious *volkish* predilection to think of a Jew—Freud or any other Jew—first and foremost only as a Jew, and so as Other, always profoundly different from "us." "Like him or dislike him, one never loses awareness that the person is not just a person, but a Jew" (65).

That this attitude towards Jews was all but universal in Europe (and the United States) before the end of World War II does not excuse it. But I sense a context in this book that Jung, Eliade, and Campbell were different. And I guess that is what puzzles me.

By 1936, Jung more or less came to the realization that the Nazis were cynically using his writings as propaganda for their cause (as they did to Nietzsche and Hegel), selectively citing some passages while banning his books and articles that were critical of their regime. Elwood cites Laurens Van Der Post's defense of Jung that "His warnings against events in Germany became more frequent, urgent, and unqualified, ending in such outright condemnation that when the war broke out his own books were banned in Germany, and he himself was placed on the Nazi blacklist for liquidation at the first opportunity" (66). And Elwood adds, "To the enigma of C. G. Jung and National Socialist totalitarianism, honesty permits no simple answer" (66).

Jung clearly lived under the illusion of Switzerland as a sacred oasis from mass man Germany, Russia, and the United States. He thought of it as a bastion of good old conservative values, and in some papers he even boasts of how the Swiss are free of the foulness and guilt of their German neighbors, a point that does not sit well today even with the Swiss themselves. But let's not go overboard here. Elwood cites a passage from Frank McLynn's 1996 biography of Jung which says, "To understand Carl Gustav Jung one must first understand Switzerland, and that is no easy matter... Superstitious, xenophobic, conservative, earthbound, introverted, moneyminded—all these epithets have been used to describe Jung, and even more frequently to describe his country" (74). But the same epithets (and worse) have been used to describe England. It is easy to get caught up in nation-bashing once you get started, and let's face it, every nation on earth has some explaining to do, especially if it is not your own.

Which brings us to Joseph Campbell, who was reportedly not only anti-Semitic, anti-Catholic (having been born one), anti-Christian, anti-Islamic, anti-African, anti-Communist, anti-feminist, and anti-hippy, but also anti-British. Most of these charges—beginning with Brendan Gill's *New Yorker*-ish resentment for bestselling authors who vote Republican and extending right up to the girl at Sarah Lawrence who said Campbell flunked her because she was an anti-Vietnam War activist—are simply the voices of our current Political Correctness. Campbell certainly was anti-Communist, as were Jung and Eliade, a matter still resented today by those fools who were not. He was also (as was Eliade) an avid Boy Scout. Traveling to Germany in the late 1920s and 1930s, he delved into the works of Oswald Spengler, the so-called "historian" of the West's decline, as well as of Thomas Mann, Nietzsche, the cultural anthropologist Leo Frobenius, and others whom he would soon be teaching in his first courses at Sarah Lawrence (where he stayed for forty years).

But Campbell's passion was for the mythology behind the world's institutionalized religions, a mythology that was eternally returning in life no matter how much religions literalized, distorted, or disguised it. "It is the purpose of the present book," he wrote in his landmark 1949 study, *The Hero With A Thousand Faces*, "to uncover some of the truths disguised for us under the figures of religion and mythology by bringing together a multitude of not-too-difficult examples and letting the ancient meaning become apparent of itself" (Elwood, 143). Academic anthropologists and folklorists have come to hate the book for the usual reasons. The literate public ate it up. Elwood cites one Marxist critic who deplored the book's "neglect" of social problems[!] and sums up this still all too prevalent view of it:

> The universalizing and psychoanalytic study of myth in the Campbell mode would, from this perspective, undoubtedly represent its appropriation by bourgeois consciousness; the latter, in marxist eyes, tends to subjectivize and aestheticize myths and stories that had their real roots in social alienation and economic deprivation. (145)

What he should have said is that the Marxist critic privileges alienation stories as "aesthetic," otherwise the Marxist critic (I like Elwood's use of the non-capital "m" in "marxist," and I hope it is not just the bad proofreading) could not care less about—or even recognize—aesthetic pleasure.

The problem was that Campbell, whose orientation—gods bless him—was always literature, never fell prey to social science. He read myths for meaning. James Joyce, who did the same, was his specialty. How furious Campbell would be, were he at Sarah Lawrence or elsewhere in academia today, to see how social science (and its virus of political correctness) has triumphed over—indeed suppressed—any other view of the arts and humanities, especially the aesethetic one. Not even literature itself is read his way anymore. Yet thanks mostly to Campbell, the study of myth became an actual course in enlightened literature departments throughout the country.

In this same context it is amusing to read Elwood's rather straight-faced account of Campbell's first trip to India, in 1954 and 1955, only after he had finished ten years of editing the papers of Heinrich Zimmer, a great Indologist and refugee from Hitler's Germany who died prematurely in New York and who wrote *The King and the Corpse*, *Philosophies of India*, and *The Art of Indian Asia*, among others. Nothing in India, Campbell wrote to his wife, "was quite as good as the India I invented" (147). Homer could have said the same of Troy. Elwood comments:

> But much of India was highly unsuitable to one of Campbell's values and temperament. Most infuriating to

> him were the ubiquitous and persistent con men and self-appointed guides and attendants, all clamorous for baksheesh. On top of that, he had to deal with the officious but inefficient bureaucracy, and to listen to tirades from intellectuals claiming that the United States—not even Britain—was somehow responsible for India's problems. At the same time India was, at this moment, enamored with socialist visions and the idea of friendship with the Soviet Union and the communist bloc. All this definitely hit a sore spot in the devoutly anticommunist mythologist.

Campbell differed from both Jung and Eliade, neither of whom could be said to have believed in human progress, and in Jung's case, emphatically not, as spoken and written on many occasions. So when Swami Nikhilananda pronounced the romantic Indian cliché that "there is no progress, only change," Campbell, I am happy to discover, shot back, "I used to think that too, Swamiji, but since coming to India I have changed my mind. I think there is progress, and I think India will begin to experience progress too, pretty soon" (147). The Campbell that had been to the real India called Gandhi—whom Eliade adored—and his disciples "primitivists" whose "alienation from the inevitables of modern life makes for a kind of romantic escapism" (147).

But while Campbell was jolted back from this aspect of his own early romanticism, he still shared with Jung and Eliade the notion that the modern world was the problem and that myth study was the solution. Campbell, Elwood says,

> prided himself on not really being part of the modern world. He never watched television and had no interest in popular culture. (Eliade, too, incidentally, during the Chicago years when I knew him, never read newspapers or sat in front of a TV and had virtually no awareness of what was happening in the outer world.) (151)

There were other gaps, most of all in his misreading of Judaism. For some reason, his ability to read myth as literature stopped here. Campbell once argued with the celebrated theologian Martin Buber over the Biblical Abraham's willingness to sacrifice his son Isaac to Yahweh. "Whatever the rights or wrongs of the argument," Elwood says, "it is apparent that examples of what Campbell considers bad religion often seem to involve Judaism and its progeny. The return from East to West did not necessarily mean a return to *these* religions"

(153). But as I read Campbell, he was neither leaving nor returning to religion, good or bad; he was interpreting the mythology of the world as if it had a reality of its own. Elwood becomes exasperated for Campbell particularly valued individualism in pagan heroes but apparently hated it in Jewish/Catholic ones. "Anyone who, despite great learning," Elwood scolds,

> could so forget both the ruthless and repressive sides of tribal paganism, and the stunning examples of Jewish and Christian individualistic heroes from David to Jesus, to embrace such a simplistic view of European culture, is beyond rational argument. (153)

It may or may not be the failure Elwood proclaims, but I think it has more to do with Campbell's general literalism as a reader—a strong reader—than with his biases. Campbell's immense value and attractiveness as a myth critic was precisely his old-fashioned insistence on meaning in myth, not the structuralist (Levi-Strauss) insistence that the medium is the message and a message only for the locals who tell it. But the trap in finding literal meaning in any religious myth is that you can easily lose sight of the imaginative nature of the genre itself. Taking myth as literature, and also taking myth as religion—both of which were Campbell's game—run the risk of forgetting sometimes that there are authors behind everything. In the case of Judaism and Abraham, one forgets the "J-author"[1] who invented the first books of the *Bible*; in the case of Jesus, one forgets the author of the "Gospel of Mark." Structuralism denies authors altogether (the current academic/socialist literary cult of "the death of the author"), while Campbell championed them—at least usually. In this case he seems to have missed an awfully big one: he does not seem to have considered, or known, (or cared?) that the *Bible* was composed by authors with personalities.

The problem with prejudice is that it distracts you from larger pleasures that you cannot see are there. The *Bible* is so integral to the Western Canon of literature (which I am a believer in, especially now when it is under such stupid assault), a literature that is so pleasurable as to be virtually the ineffable meaning of life for some of us, that using it as a foil against your other favorite world myths is just sophomoric, and certainly counterproductive. Where was Campbell's head if not his heart?

[1] Harold Bloom, *The Book of J* (Grove Weidenfeld: New York, 1990).

Nonetheless, whatever their degrees of anti-Semitism, the politics of Jung and Campbell was never fascist. Neither one of them marched to any totalitarian tune. In the case of Eliade, it is different. He did.

A native of Romania, Eliade had been a newspaper columnist, a novelist, a lecturer at the University of Bucharest, a fierce political activist before becoming an exile, and a professor at the Sorbonne and at the University of Chicago. Author of *Rites and Symbols of Initiation*, *The Sacred and the Profane*, *The Myth of the Eternal Return*, and other books, his ideas have been highly influential in the background of Jungian thought and even more so in the History of Religions movement started at Eranos with Gershom Scholem and Henry Corbin.[2] Elwood finds it hard to reconcile the "detached scholar" with whom he studied at Chicago to "the tumultuous youth of the Romanian thirties."

> This brings us to the problematic story of Eliade's relationship to the Legion of the Archangel Michael, a political/spiritual movement with fascist and anti-Semitic leanings powerful in Romania during the thirties. The Legion came to be better known as the pro-Nazi and virulently anti-Semitic Iron Guard influential in Romania's tilt toward the Axis powers in 1940 to 1941, and associated with numerous atrocities of that period. (82)

Eliade was arrested and imprisoned for his work with the Legion. His nationalistic newspaper articles, calling for "Romanianism" and a "Romania for Romanianism," wanted to curb the role of minorities there, including Jews. Elwood describes Eliade's "growing disillusionment with democracy" at this time,

> not only with what passed for democracy in his homeland, but with the idea generally. As his thought developed in this ominous direction, political and "mystical" dimensions of revolution became more and more mixed, and while Eliade always professed to esteem nonviolent, truly "spiritual" methods of combat and renewal both individually and nationally, it became increasingly easy for him to overlook lapses on this point by those he believed genuinely dedicated to the right goals. (86)

---

[2] See Steven M. Wasserstrom, *Religion After Religion: Gershom Scholem, Mircea Eliade, and Henry Corbin at Eranos* (Princeton: Princeton UP, 1999), a book I intend to review for *Spring's* next issue.

Before long he was writing admiringly of Mussolini and calling for "a new aristocracy" of the Legion. It is a dismal story, because of course we know the ultimate horror that such rhetoric led to.

Elwood's narrative of Eliade's political life, which included his later (rather unconvincing) denouncement of fascism, is fascinating, particularly the murder in 1991 at the University of Chicago of Ion Culianu, a protégé of Eliade and his literary executor, who was killed, Elwood speculates, "at the hands of Guardist elements still lingering in the murky world of Romanian politics" (95). On the other hand, does not Elwood share Eliade's and Culianu's (and the world's) loathing of the despicable Ceaucescu regime? It is perhaps too late for the city of Bucharest, mauled by socialist architecture and urban redevelopment, or for the unbelievable treatment of its citizens (most notoriously the children found in the orphanages in conditions worse than zoo animals when Western journalists finally got in). How can Elwood maintain such a dispassionate tone throughout this book? Doesn't he have any politics of his own, or is he just another unconscious liberal academician?

Elwood tries to answer a question that Culianu himself proposed concerning Eliade: "How much can we excuse a mythologist or historian of religion for, like most humans, not possessing absolute precognition, while still blaming them for not reading aright the signs of the times?" (95). But they did read aright the signs of the times in many ways. This book would be better if Elwood told us what his own political biases are—it really seems he is not aware of them—but it ought to be spelled out in a book of this kind. Too many intellectuals—especially the French—hate Jung, Campbell, and Eliade because they were anti-socialist.

Yet I find it impossible as well to accept Elwood's argument that his subjects were not idealizing myth. "For Eliade no more than for Jung was 'the primitive' idealized; it was merely different, in some ways embodying a consciousness better able to understand, and thereby to yearn for, the primal paradises of myth" (99). Merely different?

It is true that Eliade's books claim to unmask mythology (what he means by the "camouflages of the sacred in the modern") rather than disguise it further. But Jung's mystical Protestantism, Eliade's paradise of the sacred, and even Campbell's "bliss" all have in common one other thing, which this book certainly makes clear: their paradise of myth didn't have any Jews in it. I do not mean literally. All three of these profoundly gifted thinkers had Jewish friends and associates, some of them quite distinguished. That is never the point. I mean imaginatively. All three seem to have missed the most significant religious people of the twentieth century—the Jews—the people to whom the twentieth century happened.

It has nothing to do with Yahweh versus Christ, or Judaism versus other people's mythologies, or even because so many Jewish intellectuals were marxists. It is a question of missing the whole Jewish imagination itself. Yes, Freud is always lurking somewhere in their thoughts—both Jung and Campbell were, after all, full Freudians in their youth. But the Jewish imagination eclipses Freud, and a paradise without Jews is about as interesting as Philadelphia on a Saturday at 5 o'clock (if I may borrow W. C. Fields' impeccable description of what was worse than being in his grave).

Where, for just one, is Kafka, in so many ways the most indicative and precise mapper of the twentieth century's imagination and certainly its greatest gnostic—the Kafka who influenced every Jewish original in the century, from Gershom Scholem to Walter Benjamin, and most intelligent non-Jewish ones as well, from Beckett to Borges—the Kafka whose personal motto was "Never Again Psychology!" and who for that reason alone should have caught their attention—the Kafka whose own evasions of traditional Judaism (he couldn't believe, he said, in a God who was too funny for him) opened the path to a new vision of the self for everyone, a chaotic, ironic, paradoxical self that certainly exceeds anything we read in Freud or Jung. Kafka, an infinitely shrewder reader of the "Book of J" than Joseph Campbell any day, was the spiritual authority *par excellence* of the twentieth century. (Jung does not even seem to have heard of him.) The wit and irony of Kafka—so embedded in our world that it is dangerous if not impossible to read life without it—is what I miss most not only in Jung's imagination but in so much of the Jungian tradition (unless Scholem can be said to be part of that tradition).

But is not all of this—the politics of myth as the Jung/Eliade/Campbell generation presented it—one of the reasons why so many of us who still believe there is meaning in myth now call ourselves post-Jungian and even post-archetypal? Is this not where James

Hillman comes in, revisioning psychology's path out of so many of these problems, and not just reinventing an "Old Testament" to Jung's "New" but expanding the ideas into a *schule* of cultural psychology? In one of his most neglected articles, Hillman asked a question of his own work: "How Jewish is Archetypal Psychology?"[3] After tracing the Protestant, Catholic, and pagan side of his re-invention, he then addressed its own missing link, and concluded,

> The Jewish component has been forgotten—or repressed. Nothing surprising here, especially in view of the ugliness surrounding the Freud/Jung fights about "Jewish" psychology, and also how the "Jewish question" runs through all the development of and suppression of psychoanalysis.[4]

Hillman's great move, amongst many, was to show psychotherapy (Freudian and Jungian) the unconscious Christianism of its thought. "I have been trying for years to distance an archetypal psychology from the Christianism of therapy," he writes. And just as Kafka revealed the unconscious Jewishness in European culture, Hillman's archetypal psychology (for it is an issue of universalism versus particularism after all, though quite the contrary of what academic mythologists today have pulled back from) reveals the Kafkaesque in all psychology:

> Archetypal psychology does just what anti-Semitic legends have said about the Jews for centuries. It curiously conforms with vicious stereotypes that pervade the collective culture. What could be worse than to be unconscious about itself, its own Jewishness! How better court disaster than by unwittingly fulfilling the facile stereotypes of anti-Semitism? For, yes archetypal psychology does disturb the mindless life, its long nose does sniff shadows in the nice day. And tho' it appeals to the roots of Western traditions in Greece, the Renaissance and the Romantics, and revivifies these roots by revisioning them, nonetheless it takes down the high moralism, the other-worldliness, and the redemptive mission—the Christian ambition in that tradition. Archetypal psychology insidiously permeates Western faith in hope, salvation and the monotheism of love (love conquers all) which it psychologizes as styles of Christian denial.[5]

---

[3] "How Jewish Is Archetypal Psychology?" *Spring 53*, 1992, 121-130.

[4] *Ibid.*, 122.

[5] *Ibid.*, 123.

He cites *Freud's Own Cookbook*, which he and Charles Boer wrote in 1985, as an example of how this "Jewish" psychology "undermines the theologies on which it depends, biting the very hands that feed it" (including Jung's and Corbin's) and says "it tries to employ the classic Jewish rhetorics of attack" (scholarly references to authority, "twisted midrashic interpretations" and humor).[6] But all of Hillman's books make these moves and not just his send-up of Freud.

Consider only Hillman's "revision" of anima.[7] Hardcore Jungians of the old school to this day either do not understand it or condemn it as—what else?—"heretical." With its facing page selections from Jung matched by Hillman's "commentaries," the reader of that book is inside a Kafka novel. On one side of the page you have Jung as hopeless straight-man, pitching his nineteenth-century *hausfrau* dictates of what "the feminine" represents, and saying things like:

> The anima…is the "energy of the heavy and the turbid"; it clings to the bodily fleshly heart. Its effects are "sensuous desires and impulses to anger." "Whoever is sombre and moody on waking…is fettered to the anima." (*CW 13*, § 57)

Next to this you have Hillman, almost out of breath, desperately *schlepping* to the Castle, with a million qualifications that must be made:

> Syndromes current when Freud began psychoanalysis are less current today; the anima as a syndrome of excessive or inferior feminine traits is less evident as the culture moves toward incorporation of "typically anima" attitudes into its collective values. We should therefore not identify a *description* of the anima in a rigidly patriarchal, puritanically defensive, extravertedly willful and unsoulful period of history with her *definition*.[8]

I laugh, because Jung's was no more an "unsoulful period of history" than our own just politically different. But I am rooting for our great soulmeister all the way. Hillman is Kafka being Hillman reading Jung, which is the only way, personally, that someone of my own feminist persuasion can take the sage of Zürich. I was first a reader of *Re-Visioning Psychology*, the first psychology book that had

---

[6] *Ibid.*

[7] James Hillman, *Anima: An Anatomy of a Personified Notion* (Woodstock, Conn.: Spring Publications, 1985; rpt. 1996), 13.

[8] *Ibid.*, 12-13.

anything to say that I could not find in Shakespeare. (I know that sounds dumb, but I was a school teacher all my life.)

The Politics of Myth should have read the unconscious repression of its subjects' own Jewishness in the same way Hillman read it when he invented archetypal psychology. But alas, Elwood's very point of address, in this otherwise valuable study, is from the same unconsciously monotheistic perspective that is now reacting so strongly against Jung in other books coming our way. It is not that Jung, Eliade, or Campbell were anti-Semitic. It is that their work, profound as it is, would have been so much richer had they been able to address us all as the imaginary (Kafkan) Jews we have had to become—polytheistic ones to be sure, heretical absolutely, gnostic to the darkest quarter of the universe and as secular as television and email.

Book Reviews

Ann Ulanov and Barry Ulanov. *The Healing Imagination.* Einsiedeln: Daimon, 1999. Pp. 185. Paper, $17.95.

A significant and satisfying contribution to the efforts of those who, following James Hillman, seek to restore the imagination to its rightful place in the world of ideas. The Ulanovs remind us that living the well-imagined life means constant motion between outer and inner realities, opening a space of creative mediation where transformation and therapy can occur:

> In some way, whether we deliberately bring images to mind or not, the imagination is alive in us, stretching, reaching out to what has been called the All of Reality. However little we may be schooled in the interior life, however unwilling we may be to accept the existence of a deeper presence in our selves, it is there, and the agency of the imagination, primary and secondary both, constantly asserts the fact that it is so. Our subjectivity, our ego-life, by its familiar habits of operation insists on something larger than itself, some indwelling signification of being to which, like it or not, we give assent simply because we are sentient beings, because we can touch, taste, smell, hear, see, and bring to the experience of the senses the corroboration of mind that comes in image and judgment.

* * *

Christopher Elphis and Hester McFarland Solomon, eds. *Jungian Thought in the Modern World.* New York: Free Association, 2000. Pp. 277. Paper, $16.95; cloth, $40.

A wide-ranging and well-conceived anthology which seeks to demonstrate the breadth as well as the depth of its subject, with contributions by Warren Colman, Ann Kutek, Elphis Christopher, Helen Morgan, Stephen Gross, Hester MacFarland Solomon, Michael Simpson, Jean Pearson, Christopher MacKenna, Dale Mathers, John Clay, and Geraldine Godsil. In its various sections Jungian thought is considered in relation to the individual, the collective, and the new sciences:

> Jungian thought offers a framework for conceptualising a rootedness in our biology that continues to connect us to a deep collective layer beyond the peculiarities of our own individual development. It speaks of a plurality, a pantheon of gods, which reside within the deepest layers of the human psyche with which the individual ego is in relationship through the cultural myths of the day. It does not externalise responsibility, but neither does it leave the individual ego isolated from the internal resources of the unconscious of the collective. It is a framework that holds us to our humanity, however inhumane the times appear to be, and which gives us a form of linkage with each other, but also with what has gone before and, therefore, into a future. [From Helen Morgan's essay, "Modern Western Society—The Making of Myth and Meaning"]